Larry Windes

Little Houses

(AND NOT SO LITTLE) For a Grand Life

Little Houses For A Grand Life

Tiny House Architecture For An Adventure Independent Of Location

© 2023, Larry Windes

WWW.LARRYWINDES.COM

Author: Larry Windes, WWW.LARRYWINDES.COM

Editing, Proofreading: Wiebke Tasch, Digital Authors

Layout Design: Richard Powell

Self Publishing Consulting:
Digital Authors LLC, www.digital-authors.com

Table Of Contents

PREFACE

Within the last few years, especially after the 2008 meltdown of the housing market, many Architects and designers are exploring the concept of "Little Houses." Some of these are miniature in size so that they can have wheels, attached and pulled by a bicycle.

Others have been morphed into varieties of mobile home sizes that are highway-legal in the USA. These are commendable efforts and many creative designs have resulted. The endeavors to absolutely shrink a house to the near limit have been studied for hundreds of years within the august discipline of Marine Architecture. If you want to learn how to efficiently cram the "Mostest-within-the leastest", take a look in the yacht harbor. Not only have boat designers figured out how to utilize every possible teacup of space, they take the entire package and throw it into the ocean, allow thunderous waves to smash everything, and Mom doesn't even have to straighten up after.

The objective of this book is a bit less drastic. The realization is that a "permanent" house needs to be of sufficient size to assuage the occupant's creature-comfort zone for longer than a couple of months. To this end, the smallest design deemed appropriate here is a one-bedroom cabin containing a modest 320 square feet (30 m2) of livable interior floor area. The remaining cabins, cottages and villas graduate in size to the largest more than 5000 sq.ft. (465m2). It may be argued that the largest hardly may be fairly referred to as a little house, but if you have ever visited the Middle Eastern Petrol-countries, five thousand square feet is a modest guest house. Size, however, is not the only issue. What you do with it, regardless of size, is the defining aspect of *Little Houses for a Grand Life*.

So, what do you mean by A Grand Life, you say?

We have always considered that our home is our castle. For the rich, it has been ever so. For the rest of us, this can become more than an illusion, and it is not a function of money. All that is really needed is a sense of wonder and the determination to create a life of appreciation and joy during every moment. Enrichment of place means caring about each and every aspect of one's home environment. Grand is not necessarily "big." A Grand Life is a Meaningful Life.

Hopefully, these bits of thought and visual reflections they fostered will assist you in the quest.

And to you, Cindy, my love, thank you ever so much.

Foreword

As you read and view the following numerous houses, regardless of size, one aspect herein is decidedly the same. They are all built on site as permanent buildings. In today's world, people of all walks of life are becoming more mobile, and often occupy two or three successive homes within a short time period. The Tiny House movement has offered a solution which allows portability for one's home to follow the homeowners to the next location.

The last chapter, <u>To the Future</u>, shows the author's version of a Tiny House. This tiny house not only has what typical tiny houses offer, but FAM (Fold-A-Mansion) additionally incorporates numerous aspects that are sorely lacking within thousands of other tiny houses throughout the world. What is that you say?

Nearly all other Tiny Houses are extremely narrow and claustrophobic. FAM is more than 20 feet (6 meters) wide and spacious. Nearly all other Tiny Houses have no roof overhangs, a big problem within harsh weather locations. <u>FAM</u> has a minimum of 2 feet (60 centimeters) roof overhangs surrounding most exterior walls and porches. Nearly all Tiny Houses have sleeping lofts, but usually only a meager 3 feet (90 centimeter) clearance under the upper roof. FAM has a "POP-UP" roof over the loft with 5'6" (168 centimeters) clearance under the upper roof plus 7 windows facing in all directions. No Claustrophobia.

Added to this, the FAM concept embraces the unique opportunity for nearly any COMMERCIAL, INSTITUTIONAL, or CULTURAL occupational use of similar size to occupy a <u>FAM.</u>

This means that virtually any business, I.E. Coffee Shop, Office, school, Church, Studio, Resort etc. You can follow the owner to the next location. Your FAM tiny house and small business help you to make your dream come true. You can work from anywhere, where you are offering your high-end service and be independent from seasons, weather, and locations.

Your Grand Life is just a tiny <u>FAM</u> away.

Chapter I

Illustrations

All the illustrations within this book have been conceptualized, designed, and drawn personally by the author. Although thousands of precedents were garnered as research, each design shown is an individual work drawn either in pencil or ink utilizing timeless drafting and rendering techniques learned and practiced over fifty years. I welcome computer-aided design and have worked with expert cad operators since the inception of the cathode ray tubes finding their way into the profession. It is a superb tool, but only a tool. The mind is what creates all Architecture, and, for the present, all designs end up on a piece of paper from which the builder executes the construction. I happen to prefer the direct hand-to-paper approach without any electronic middleman (or woman). Why is this?

Recently, a symposium was hosted that discussed the demise of drafting as an archaic method soon to disappear. Those who purport this concept obviously do not themselves know how to draw. Architectural drawing, whether sketching or mechanical drawing, is a tactile art of immense magnitude and many years are required to nurture and develop the requisite skills. The thought of throwing all this devotion away in order to play with a plastic mouse and poke a keyboard is to denigrate the spirit of hand drawing. Look closely at the drawings in this book. Compare these precise, literal, definitive drawings to the lifeless paste up renderings in any Architectural trade magazine. You be the jury.

Bella Cabin

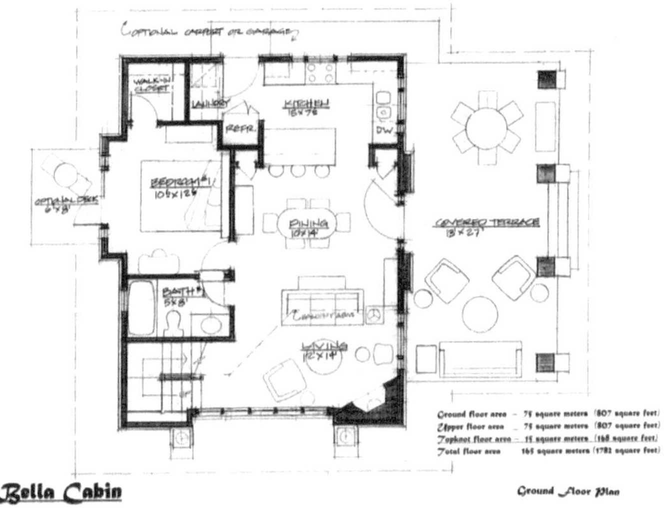

Bella Cabin

Ground Floor Plan

Bella Cabin is a three- bedroom, two- bath house with separate living areas on each floor, plus a hideaway "topknot" on the third level. All room sizes are kept to a minimum while window size and placement are intended to increase visual sense of light and air. The large front window is especially effective when the house is facing a mountainous view.

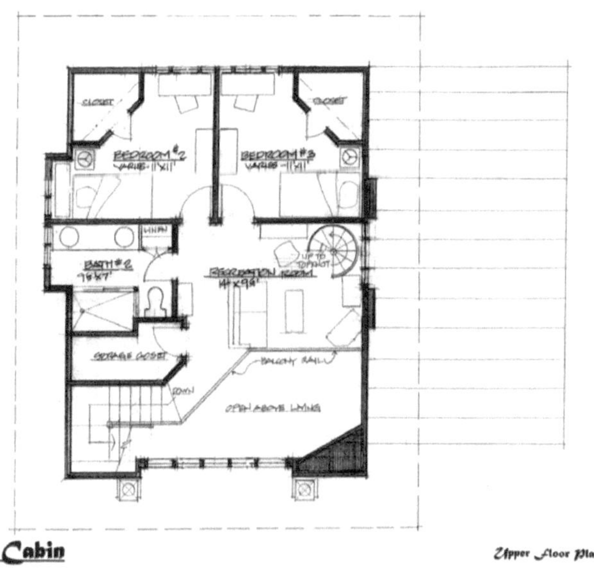

Bella Cabin

Upper Floor Plan

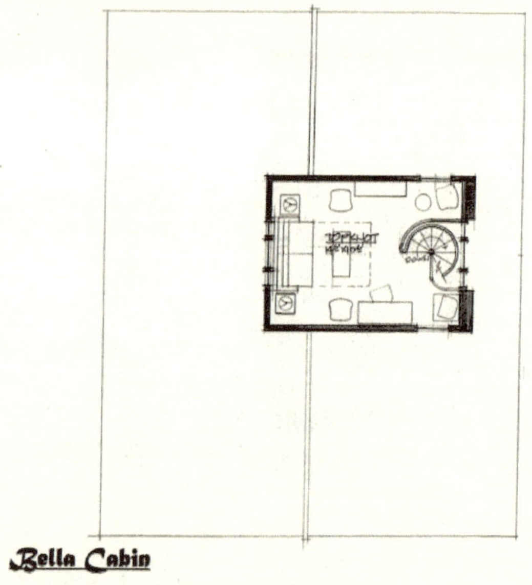

Bella Cabin

Topknot Floor Plan

The livable interior floor area totals 1782 square feet (165 square meters). A covered terrace of 350 sq.ft. (32 sq.m.) is shown on the Right-Side Elevation where a carport is also shown to accommodate a single vehicle. Although Bella Cabin was designed to be constructed of polystyrene foam covered with cement plaster on all walls, floors, roof, and foundation, the cabin may be easily built utilizing a variety of more conventional systems.

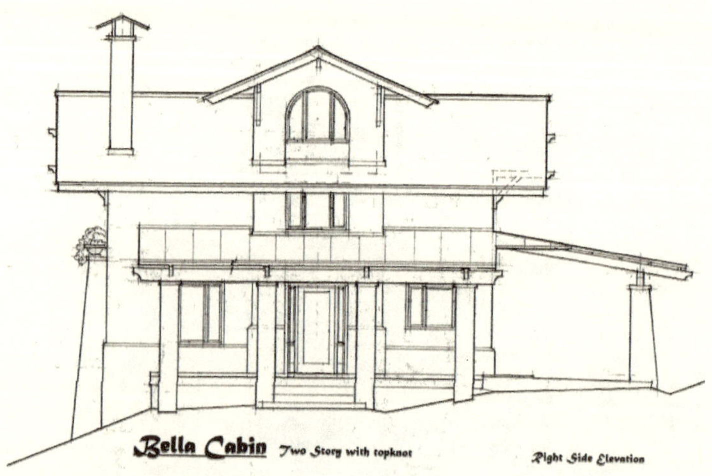

Bella Cabin *Two Story with topknot*

Right Side Elevation

Chapter 2

Introduction

In the mid-1960's, as a fledgling young Architectural student, I was about mid-term of my second year of design class when I began to sense that something seemed a bit odd. While designing a single-family house project, all the examples that we were shown as "good design" happened to be flat roofed, square shaped, and rectangular windowed with elevations that were much the same regardless of where the buildings were to be built. I had grown up in a house full of antiques and loved them all. I even liked the diamond paned windows that Mom had installed in the front room. I drew diamond windows for my project.

My professors were aghast, especially those from the East coast. "This is not contemporary!" Oops? Suffice to say, I was a quick study and within the parameters of the "contemporary" design idiom, I carried myself well and garnered good marks throughout and up until graduation. The sense that something was missing, however, never went away.

I served my apprenticeship and after gaining my registration as a licensed Architect in Colorado, USA, I set up a small practice in Aspen. Since the burgeoning ski resort was originally a wealthy silver mining town in the 1890s, there were numerous fine existing old residences of the Queen Anne version, and the remainder of the town retained a distinctive Victorian feel. Personally, it seemed an anathema to drop a "contemporary" visual carbuncle onto the town, so I began designing in a pseudo-Victorian style for numerous projects. I relished the richness of character within this and other period styles and began a lifelong course of study, traveling the world, living in foreign climes, and experimenting in my own version of multitudinous and varied Architectural expressions. Through the following five decades, the vast horizon of Architecture opened its soul and that sense of longing faded away into a joyous career without any design boundaries save that which is personally perceived to be beautiful.

This book is a compilation of observations, criticisms, conjectures, and recommendations of what Little Houses can do to, and for, one's life. There is much ado about what feels wrong within today's residential designs and no holds were barred in pointing fingers. The difference, however, is that along with laying blame, there are scores of literal examples herein of what the author offers as potential solutions to that wee bit of odd feeling rising out of contemporary residential Architecture of today.

This flamboyant High Victorian Style residence, when viewed from the exterior, appears to be from the mid 1880s yet the floor plan views show contemporary open planning.

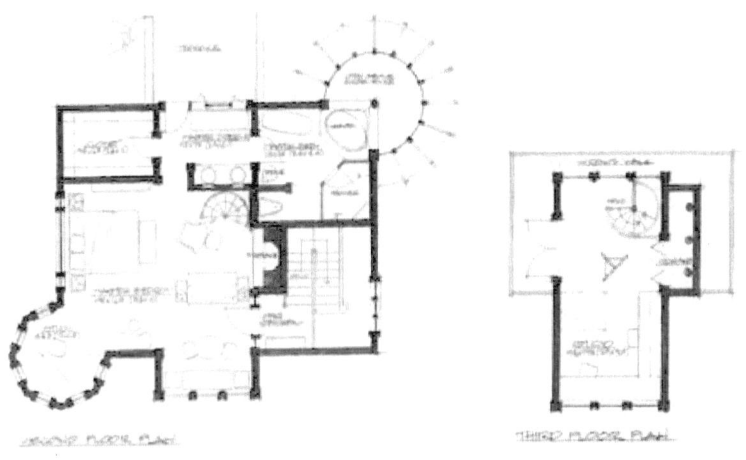

Kathryn's High Victorian

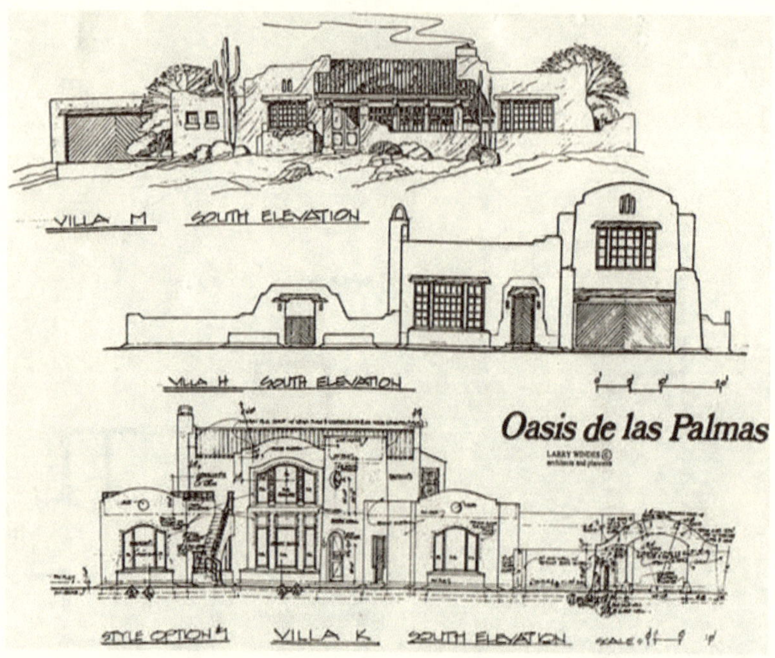

Oasis de Las Palmas is a collection of medium size houses ideally suited for location in arid climates. All are designed to include at least a two-car garage within the building envelope, but also intended for the garages not to visually overpower the principal façade of the building. All plans have extensive window areas with orientation towards semi-enclosed courtyards. Four of the plans are two-story and incorporate second floor level terraces or balconies. Exterior living areas enable multiple uses which in normal cases would only be flat rooftops. All layouts utilize the Open Plan concept which blends Living, Dining, Kitchen, and often Family rooms into a continuous spatial flow. This concept allows for a smaller overall floor area while retaining the illusion of larger spaces.

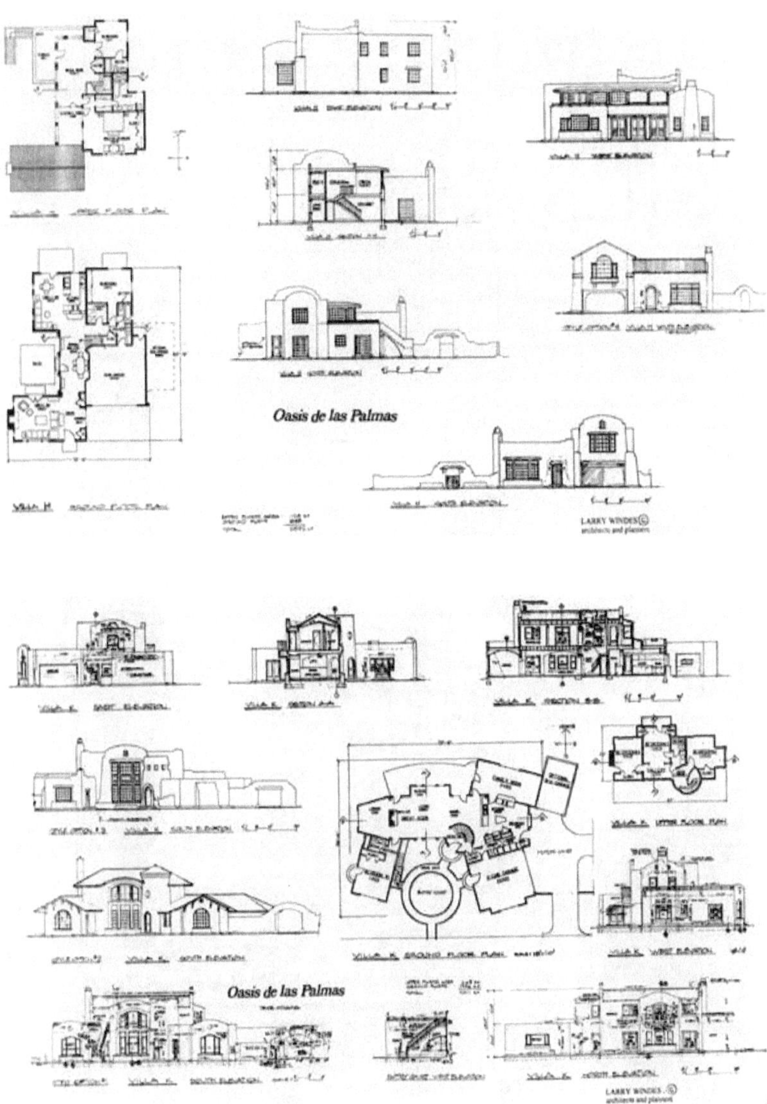
Oasis de las Palmas
LARRY WINDES
architects and planners
Oasis de las Palmas
LARRY WINDES
architects and planners

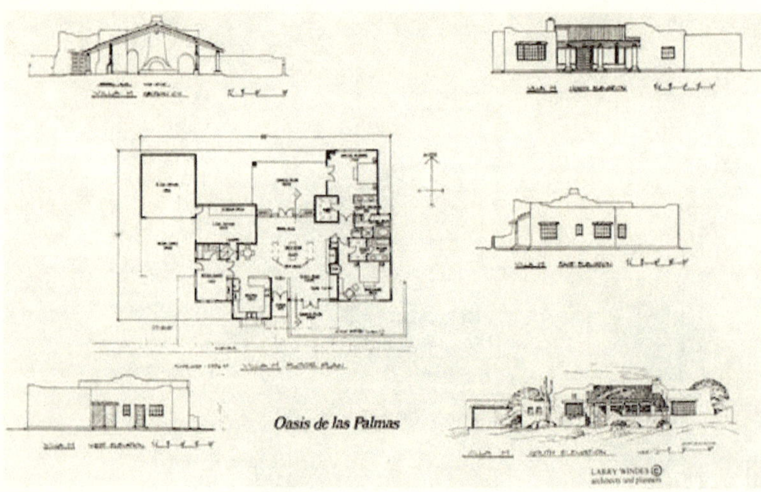

Oasis de las Palmas

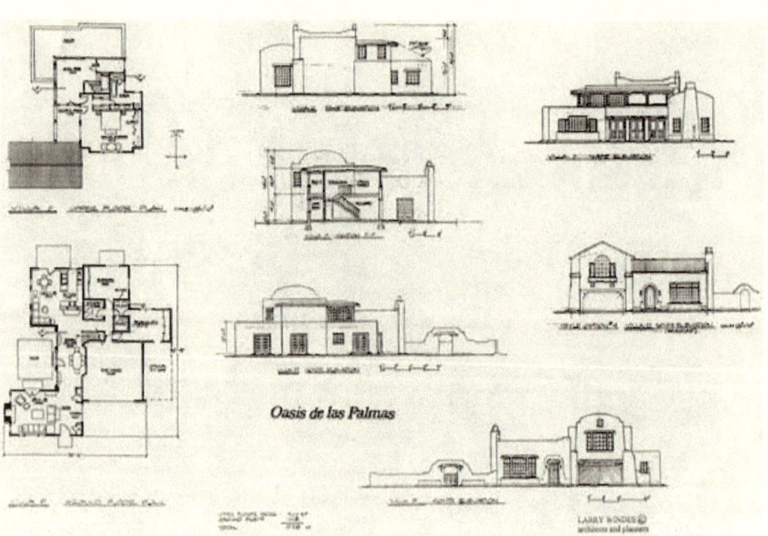

Oasis de las Palmas

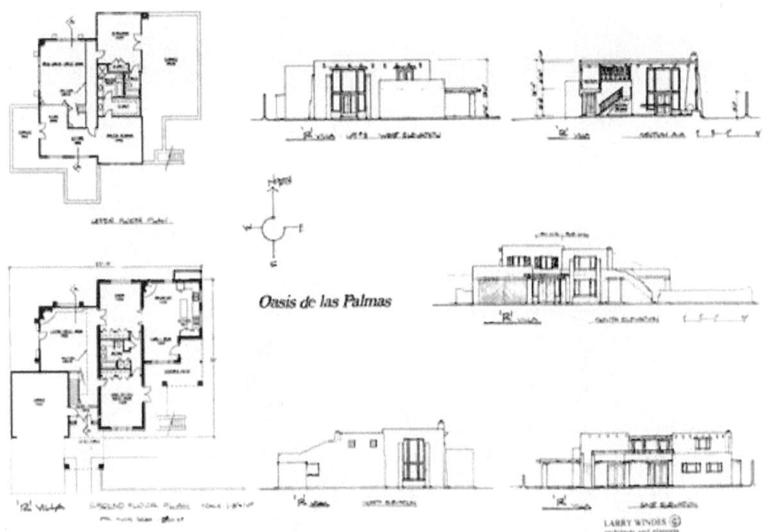

Many years ago, a grade-school friend lived in an old adobe house within a date tree orchard. The foot thick sun-dried mud walls were cool to the touch even within the hottest of Arizona summers. All was quiet and serene due to the sound absorption properties of the mud adobe, and everyone felt tranquil within. It was designed in simple Sante Fe style and using contemporary Architectural jargon of today, would be referred to as "minimalist."

Minimalism in design is thought to be understood by the layman as "use of the fewest and barest elements" thus rendering the design a sensibly simple character. Unfortunately, eighty years of Architectural dogma has resulted in a religious catechism of bare-boned boxes, stripped of any semblance of "character," reduced to cold, lifeless spaces within, then furnished with uncomfortably hard-edged surfaces. These designs are not inexpensive, they are not simple (simplistic, yes) and they have led everyone to be fooled that "God is in the details." Certainly, one cannot speak for God, but like the rest of us, undoubtedly, he has been bored to tears for decades.

Betty and her mom added soft furniture, handcrafted Navajo rugs, colorful paintings, and filled every nook and cranny with flowers. They also filled the home with caring and Love, and there is nothing "minimalist" about that, God knows.

Chapter 3

House or Home

Your friendly real estate salespersons call every house a home. They do this to convey a particular emotion that will result in a sale. Is a house a home? Not necessarily.

The vast majority of residential designs have been oriented to the tastes of women and women demand to live within a house that she can call "home." Home to them evokes something that is felt more than just seen. These feelings of home are elicited by an ephemeral mix of subtle attributes often expressed as cozy, comfortable, nurturing, and warm. These attributes are qualitative in nature and cannot be just added to a house for it to become a home. They must be blended within a symphony of feelings to become the frozen music of architecture. Sensitivity is essential to feel how every space will affect those residing within. Sensitivity is essential to convey these feelings into Architecture.

Medieval cathedrals were grand spaces which certainly created awe and a sense of humility for the parishioners. Nobody ever stayed very long in a cathedral. Where people did spend countless hours, and still do, is at the local pub, where there is invariably a low ceiling and a series of small intimate spaces. Without fail, the common-sense rule of "homeness" is that "The loftiness of the space is indirectly proportional to the coziness." Huge rooms may impress the neighbors, but nobody wants to be in them. This is especially magnified pertaining to children. Their preferred lofty space is out-of-doors which is second only to their bedroom where they can text their friends in secure privacy.

"Character" is a key to discovering Homeness and, if this is so, where is character found? Any book about house design published prior to 1930 will be an excellent place to start. Period styles from every culture were infused with character. Victorian in England, Art Nouveau in France and Belgium, the Arts & Crafts movement in New (and old) England, Santa Fe pueblos, the Belle Epoque roots in San Francisco Bay area and countless other indigenous styles worldwide exude "character." The domestic architecture of Voysey and Lutyens outside London, Guimard in Paris, Horta in Brussels, Wissa Wasif and Fathi in Cairo, Mizner in Florida, Schweinfurth, Maybeck and Straub in California are all worthy of a serious look. If time is limited to the study of only a single Architect, Frank Lloyd Wright stands alone as the greatest of the greatest twentieth century masters, having fostered dozens of "styles" within his august career. He will never bore you.

If not content to search for the essence of Home within "Old stuff," a quick look may be taken at the works of the modernist movement or of the contemporary "contexturalists." Alas, if the home is a symphony of feeling compared to a house, the modernists have uttered little more than a burp and a fart. Watch, rather, a few movies such as *Star Wars* or *Lord of the Rings* to see superb glimpses of other fantasy worlds with sufficient "character" to last more than a few lifetimes.

To summarize, the smallest house can exude more feeling than a mighty mansion, and for the greater multitudes in the coming years, a smaller house will be the default setting. Economic considerations will continue to demand less space and greater efficiency of the use of space. People will be spending more time at "home" and that will be a blessing rather than a curse. The house is where we may live, but Home is where the heart is.

Cynthia's Manor

This particular design is the result of a concerted attempt to create a blend of Old-World character one might observe in the North of France. Whereas the Entry (North) Elevation represents the restrained symmetry that is typical of Normandy a hundred fifty years ago, the South Elevation breaks with tradition with a potpourri of elements superimposed onto the central visual theme. The mandatory requirement from the client (my wife) was that this design exemplifies what it "feels like" to be a home, rather than just a house. What do you think?

The Ground Floor area of Cynthia's Manor is 1260 square feet (117 sq. meters). The Upper Floor area is 780 Sq.ft. (72 sq. m.). The optional Lower Ground Floor is 1200 sq.ft. (112 sq.m.)

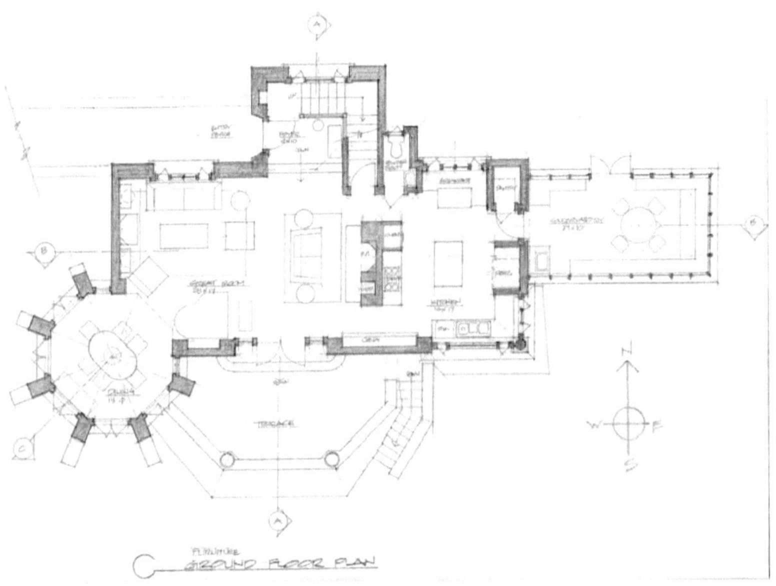

Every space is intended to have a unique character and evoke a special feeling.

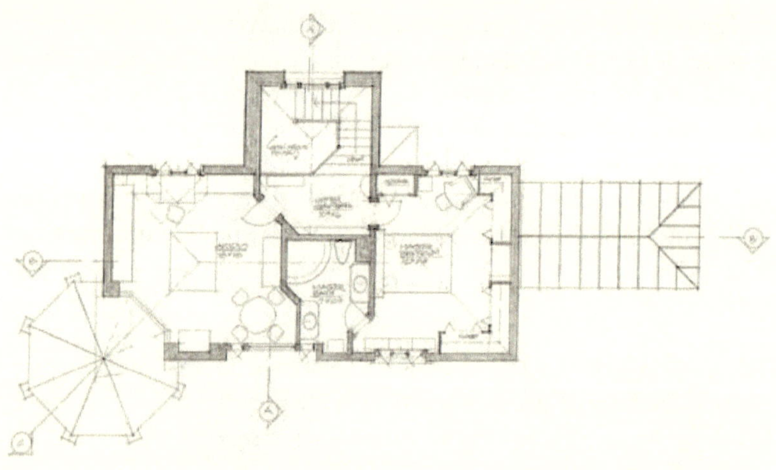

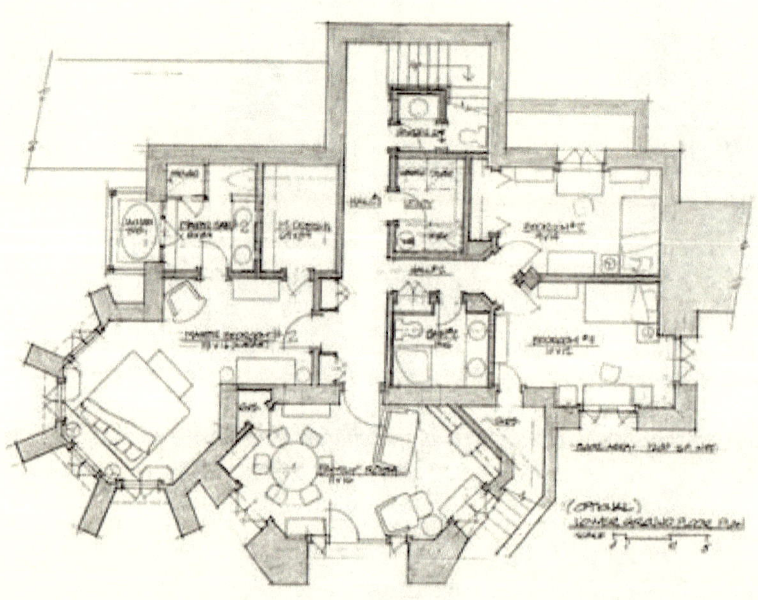

The Lower Ground Level is an option, and the windows and doors are not shown on the Elevation views.

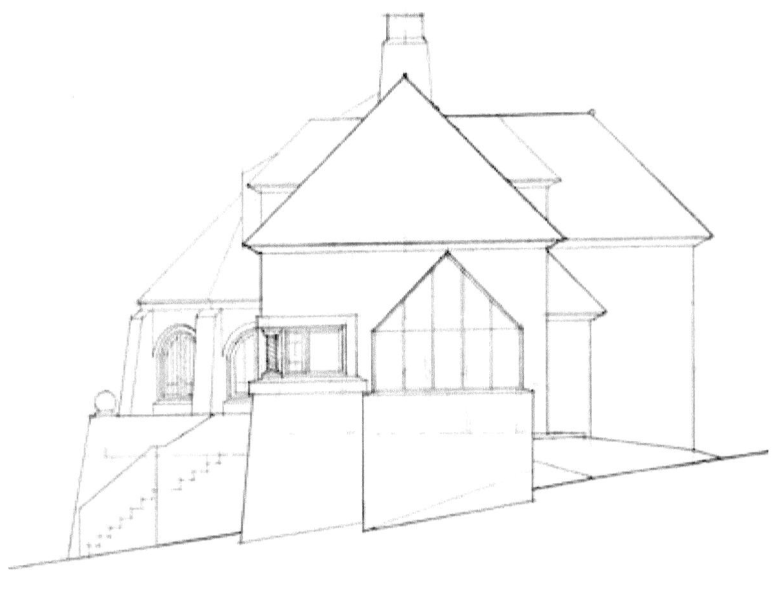

A covered arcade is shown on the right above which is an optional link to a Garage.

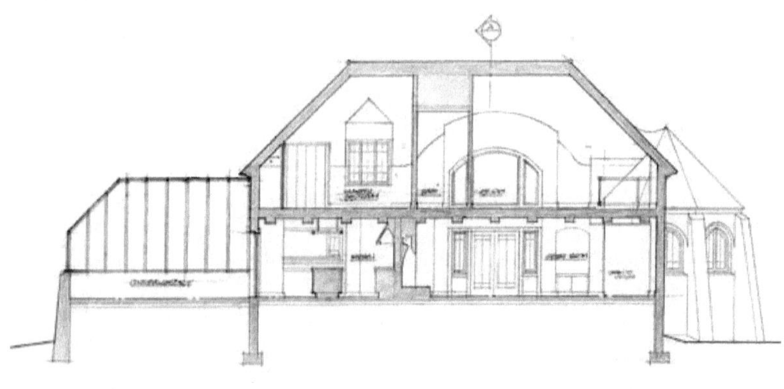

Differing ceiling heights together with windows and doors of varying height and configuration are shown here which serve to enrich the visual experience within the building.

Shown above is a cut away view of the Arcade with the arched entry door and Dining Turret beyond.

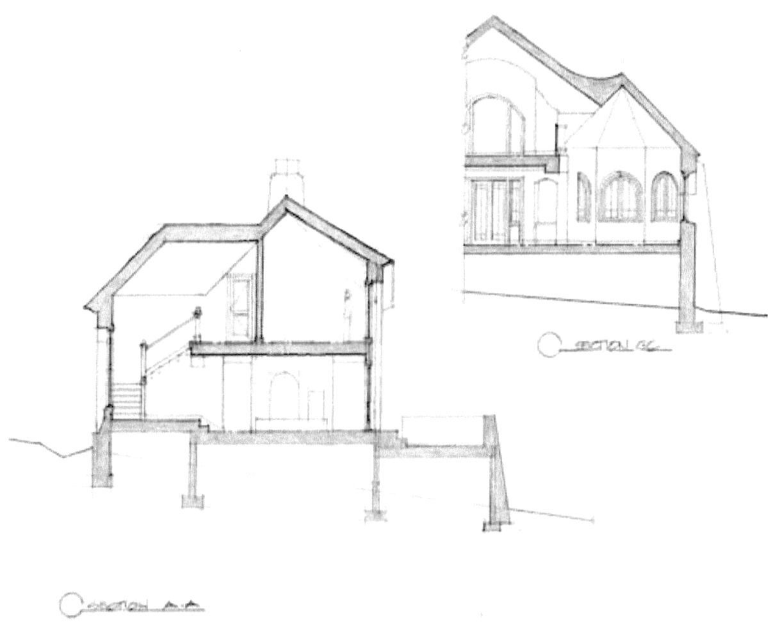

The two Sections above show the interplay of ceiling heights and spatial volumes.

Chapter 4

It's NOT a Community

The sales pitch says, "A Planned Community"! Yes, they are planned, but are they really communities? A hundred years ago, all communities from the smallest town to the largest city forced people to interact, thus enabling a night and day continuum of face-to-face

communication resulting in friendship and trust. People lived, worked, and played in the same neighborhood and thus the social fabric therein created a sense of community.

In the second quarter of the 20th century, three things occurred that began to unravel this fabric. The refrigerator allowed people not to shop daily, the automobile/truck allowed for decentralization plus lowering of population density (sprawl), and zoning regulations forced separation of use (suburbia).

The refrigerator certainly does not prevent people from shopping, they still do. For many of us, it is the only way to meet and interact with other people, save for the workplace. The refrigerator did allow for the centralization of food distribution and sales, thus moving groceries away from individual neighborhoods.

The primary enabler of "sprawl" was the auto/truck. Giving everyone the wonderful benefit of instant, easy transportation, the insidious back door was loss of density and all the social benefits of our living in a pedestrian environment. The mere "spread" of the landscape literally separates us physically and steals our much-needed time. Sprawl also consumes tremendous costs for roadways, parking facilities, and utility infrastructure to build and maintain.

The third contributor to the loss of our social fabric was probably the most damaging because it was the result of altruistic and noble objectives. When we moved next door to the cattle feed lot and rendering plant, legislation was formulated to separate uses for the common good. Unfortunately, misguided planning along with the resulting zoning regulations mandated that people could not live, work and play on the same building site. (No more store below with office and residence above). This absolute madness by law has only within the most recent few years begun to change.

These concepts and others have brought about the disappearance of the Neighborhood. The basic element of society is the family and much has been written about the demise of this American institution today. The immediately larger element of society was historically the tribe. The tribe evolved in terms of scale into the neighborhood. In 1920 nearly every neighborhood was a viable social entity, giving support to those living within immediate walking distance while allowing them to live, work, play, and be educated in familiar proximity. Virtually all "communities" that have been built since the early 1930s have been consciously deprived of the existence of neighborhoods in the social sense. Without benefit of these neighborhood building blocks, the soul-less suburban environment boasts all the numerous things (civic center, shopping mall, mega store, power center, arts district, etc.) but still is bereft of "community".

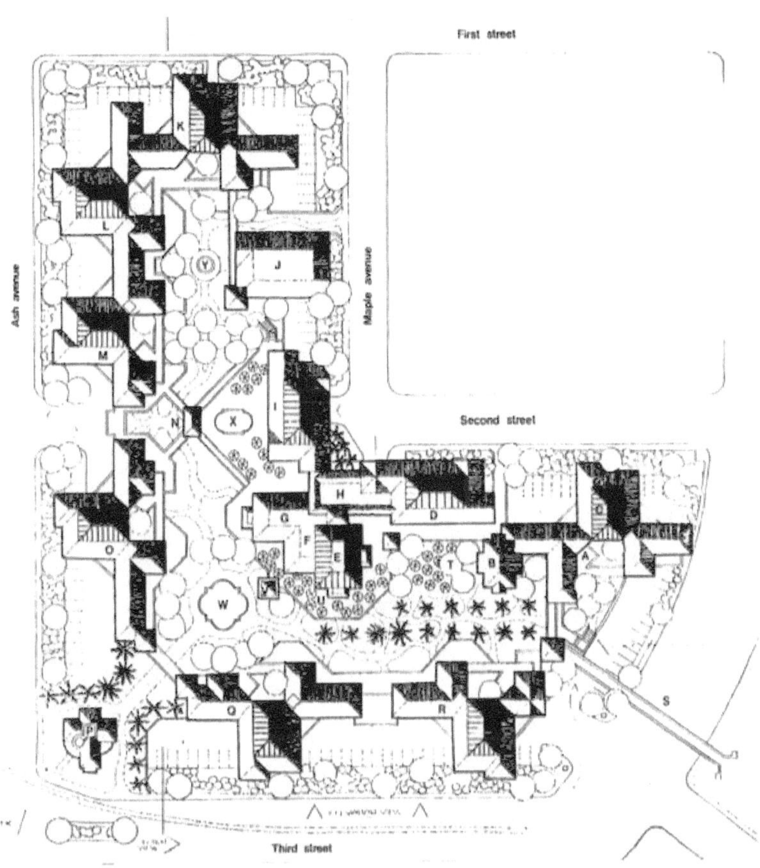

Here is a Site Plan of a true vertical mixed use "Urban Village" which satisfies the real requirements necessary for a true neighborhood to function as a viable, dynamic, and fun living environment.

SITE PLAN LEGEND

A. Commercial, Offices

B. Private Club, Offices

C. Health Spa, Commercial, Offices

D. Hotel Rooms

E. Hotel Restaurant

F. Hotel Kitchen

G. Cabaret

H. Hotel Lobby

I. Hotel Rooms

J. Conservatory and Performing Arts

K. Day Care Center, School for Special Education, Apartments

L. Branch Library, Apartments

M. Apartments

N. Mass Transit Station (below grade)

O. Apartments, Offices

P. Information and Visitors Center, Historical Exhibit, Chapel

Q. Apartments, Offices, Commercial

R. Commercial, Offices

S. Pedestrian Bridge

T. Nursery, Sidewalk Cafes

U. Outside Dining Terrace

V. Water Tower and Carillon

W. Main Plaza with Fountain

X. Hotel Swimming Terrace

Y. Performing Arts Plaza

Z. Rooftop Greenhouse Agricultural Unit

As can be seen, all primary components of Residential, Commercial, Educational, and Cultural uses are blended within a walking area less than two city blocks. All vehicular parking is below grade under the entire site. The Ground level is a pedestrian plaza surrounded by Hotel, Commercial, Recreational, and Cultural venues. The second-floor level is comprised of offices and the floors above are residential Condominiums and Apartments with rooftop gardens in greenhouses.

This layout, called Vertical Mixed Use, was the way every community was built throughout the world prior to 1900. When presented to the City for zoning approval in the mid 1970's the planning officials and Council thought we were nuts and sent us packing. Fortunately, thirty-five years later, the New Urbanism concept that followed us a decade later, has become the "new" mainstream concept.

It is fine to "pioneer" but be careful not to be too early in the game.

Chapter 5

Entitlements

In good ol' Abe Lincoln's day, when the family needed a cabin, dad chopped down a bunch of trees and built one. He never had to ask anyone for permission to do it. As towns grew into cities, densely packed wood structures tended to catch fire and with a bit of wind, the entire community went up in smoke. In order to prevent a re-occurrence, city governments initiated a code of laws defining required materials and techniques for construction along with an enforcement department of Building Inspectors. This was a good idea and also the fees charged to the building owner for a Building Permit added welcome income to the city's general fund.

When the local slaughterhouse and rendering plant became surrounded by new housing tracts, the homeowners cried foul, as in Phew! As a result, a new city department, Planning and Zoning was enacted. This group formulated a Master Plan and Zoning Code book, plus initiated another process for the new builder to comply with, along with another accompanying fee. As the years went by, these required codes became huge and ever so more complicated, to say nothing of expensive and time consuming. The building permitting process may have been a bit painful, but fortunately, the Building Code itself was specific in nature and straight forward. If the building design was complying and the construction followed the plans, there would be no problem. The inspectors approved the work and issued a certificate of occupancy.

Planning and Zoning was soon to be a different matter. In the early 1960s it was determined that the zoning regulations needed to be more "flexible" to allow for the accommodation of changing lifestyles. Planned Area Development now allowed the housing developer to submit his plans to a Zoning Commission of lay persons for approval based upon planning staff recommendations. Needless to say, this process rapidly evolved into a political nightmare forum necessitating public input and even City Council voting for even the smallest project. The suburban cities as have resulted everywhere in contemporary North America are a pathetic mess, but that particular rant is for another book at another time.

The upshot for the designing, permitting, and building of your new "Little House" is that, should you be favoring the use of one of these enclosed house plans, your Architect and builder will be readily able to implement any necessary minor modifications to comply with local codes and ordinances. As new, would-be homebuilders lurch into the third decade of the new millennium, the time and cost to endure the "entitlement process" may actually increase. Along with falling revenues, city staff will be reduced and the remaining few will likely become doubly anal in their race to prove their worth. Plan checker turf wars may commence, at least until there is no cash remaining in the general fund. Eventually, the local government employees might just have to learn how to use a shovel and become a positive addition to the common good. Eventually, chickens will finally be allowed within the limits of one's suburban back yard as a zoning concession to reality. Planning staff will likely recommend, however, that the ordinance requires that roosters wear a gag.

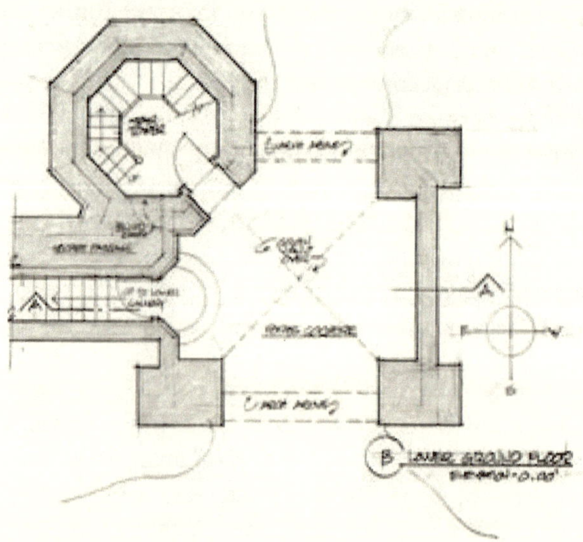

The Tower

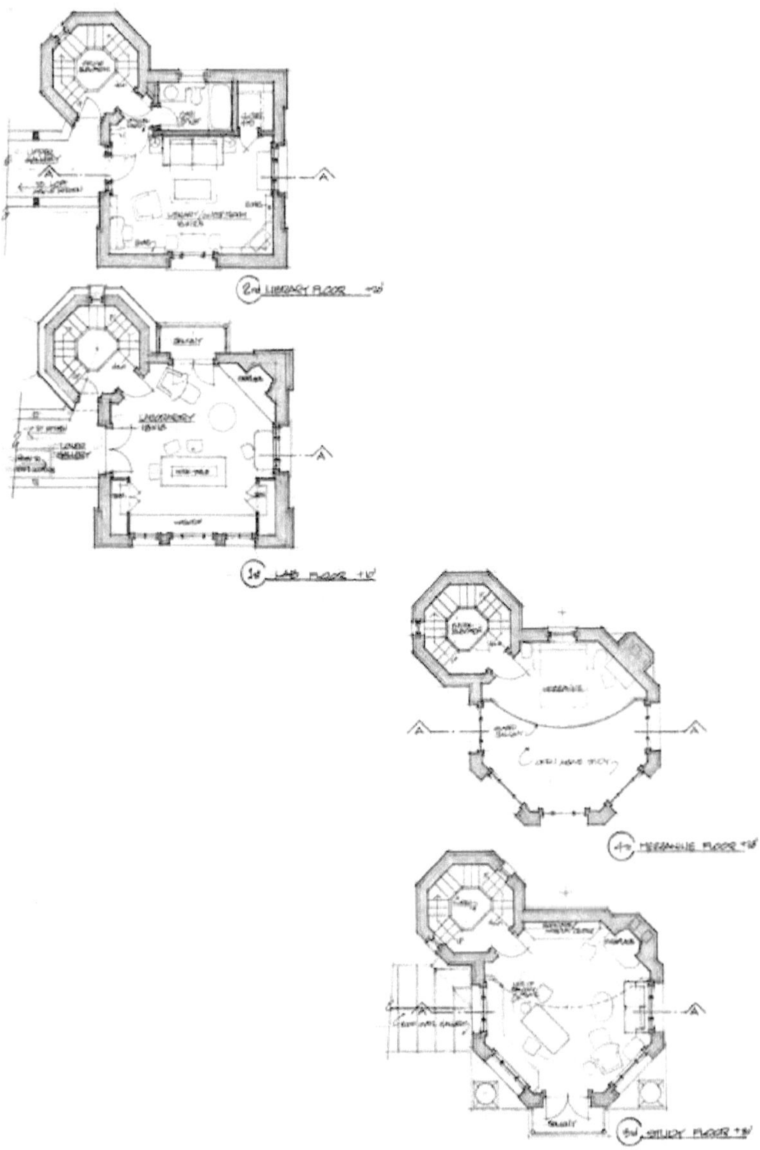

Wait a minute! The discussion was about Entitlements and all of the sudden the drawings are showing a TOWER? What gives?

What gives? There is NO what gives, that's what. There is no way that this Tower building will ever be issued a building permit within a typical residential zone. Never!

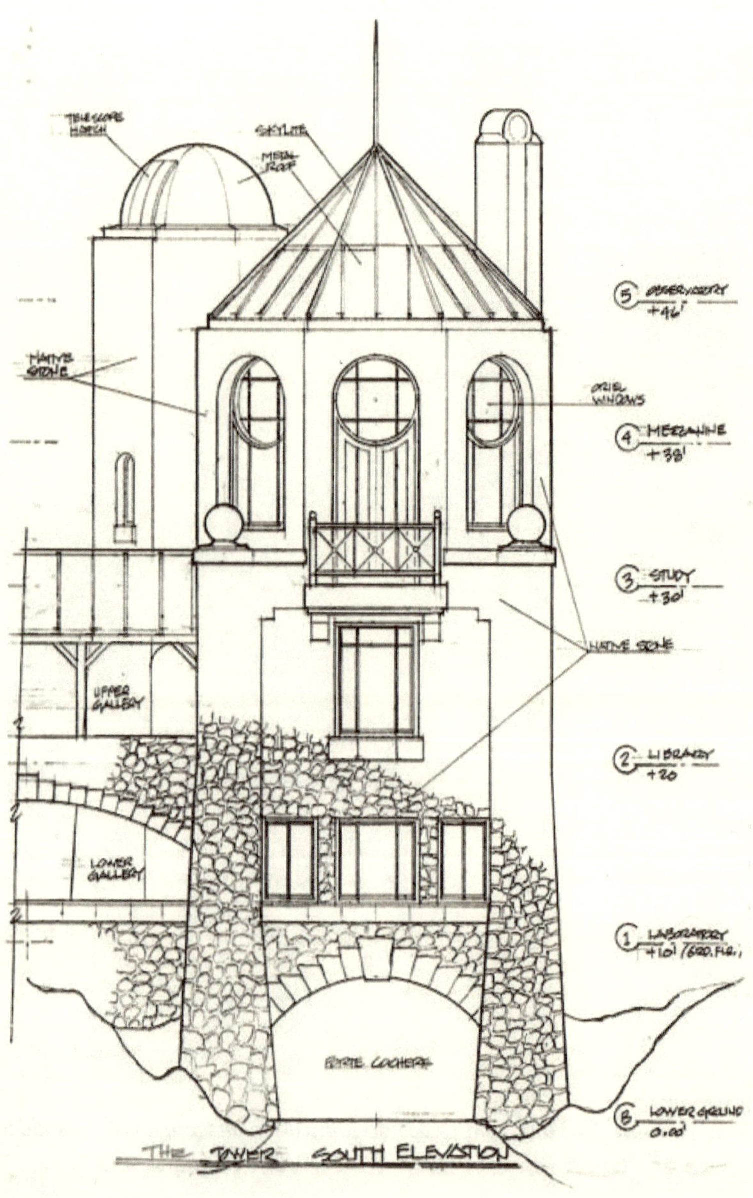

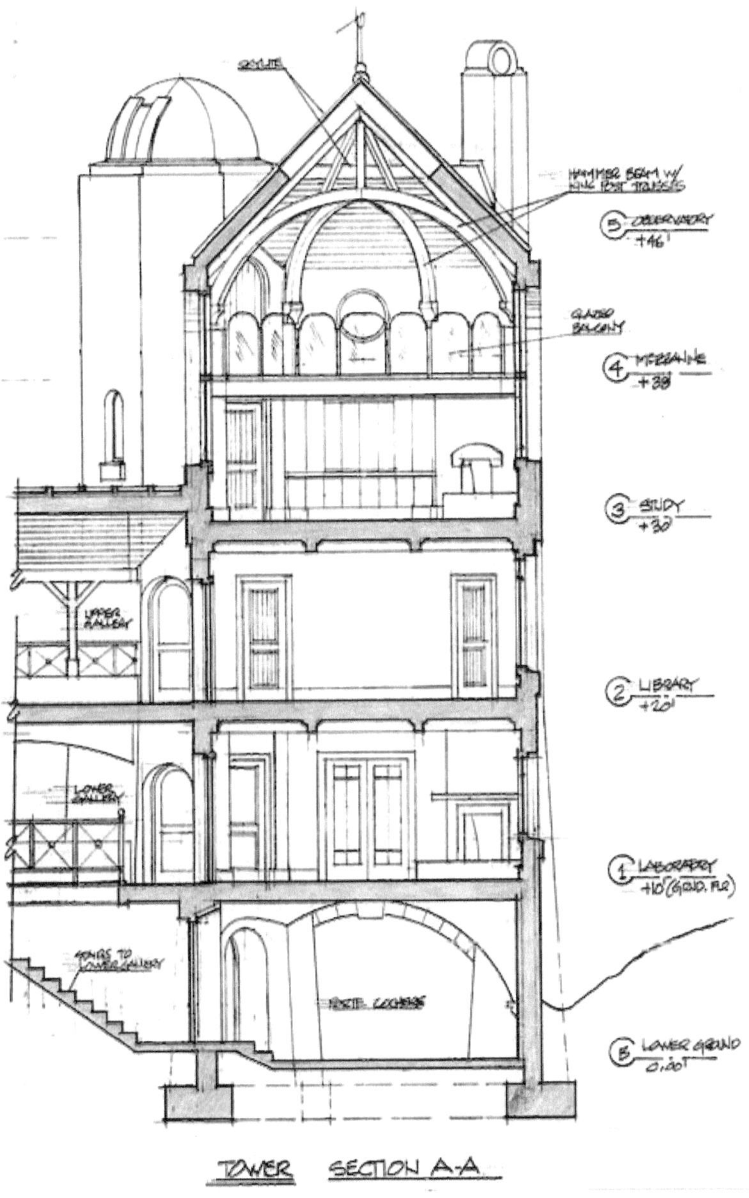

A hundred years ago you could build this "one man's fantasy" on a remote parcel of land. Today it would require high rise zoning which is usually issued to downtown areas only. Sorry.

Chapter 6

The Plot

To a subsistence farmer, it is all about plot. No, this is not a mystery. This plot is all about the piece of land where we can place a little house and commence a self-sufficient lifestyle within walking distance. The plot does not have to be a large tract of land. A typical ¼ acre (1000 sq. meters) subdivision lot, after reducing the area attributed to house, garage, and driveway remains sufficiently ample to support a family of four with veggies, fruits and flowers. This goal does, however, require planning, hard work, persistence and not a little luck, especially within harsher climate zones.

Many people are not interested in personally getting involved in gardening, preferring to outsource exterior house maintenance and landscaping. Certainly, that is their prerogative, and they will still benefit from living within a smaller house and smaller plot. One particular benefit is a reduction in property taxes. These taxes seem to be always on the increase as governments relentlessly attempt to extort the homeowner to pay for their bloated budgets. Our personal solution was to outsource ourselves to a country that demands a mere fraction of the amount attributed to this tax classification as compared to back home. The local road repair may suffer a trifle (actually it doesn't), but when one is walking, the point is moot.

When utilizing a small plot, careful site planning is essential in order to obtain the most effective use of the property. Demand that your Architect take careful heed to orientation of the living spaces, both inside and out, towards the sun. In the Northern hemisphere, rooms facing south are the best bet. The view of your house from the street is only important for the Architect's (and maybe your own) ego. If the house is properly thought out, every side will be a "front side." Exterior areas are living spaces as important as the interior of the house, and thoughtful consideration must be given to every square foot of the plot. Much definition of exterior spaces will be manifested by landscaping and the ground, wall and overhead planes will be greened transitions from building to site. If the landscape plan is holistic in concept, not only will the plants be visually appealing, but you also will be able to eat them. It requires no more effort to plant the entire landscaped area for food. It only requires a conscious master plan together with a determined execution.

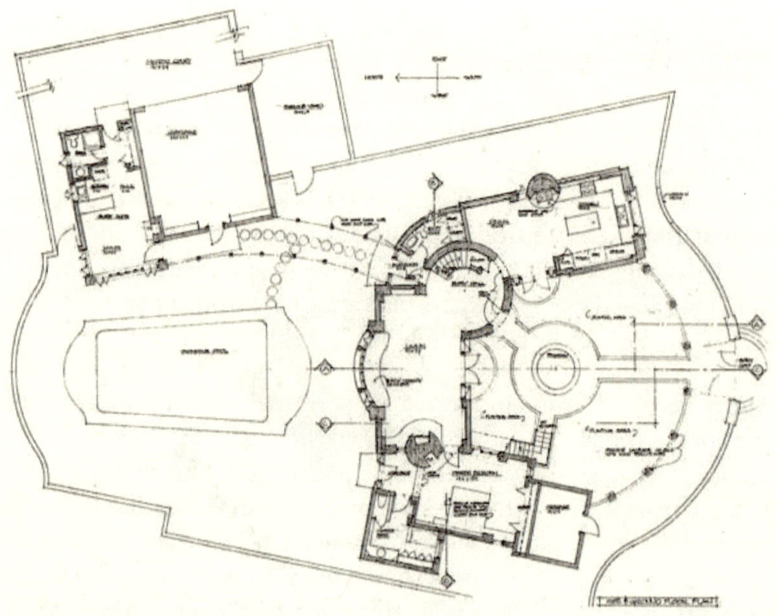

Oasis Villa

Oasis Villa has been designed to embrace the outdoors by surrounding an entry garden with fountain and extending a pergola toward the rear swimming pool. The entire site is fully landscaped within a walled enclosure.

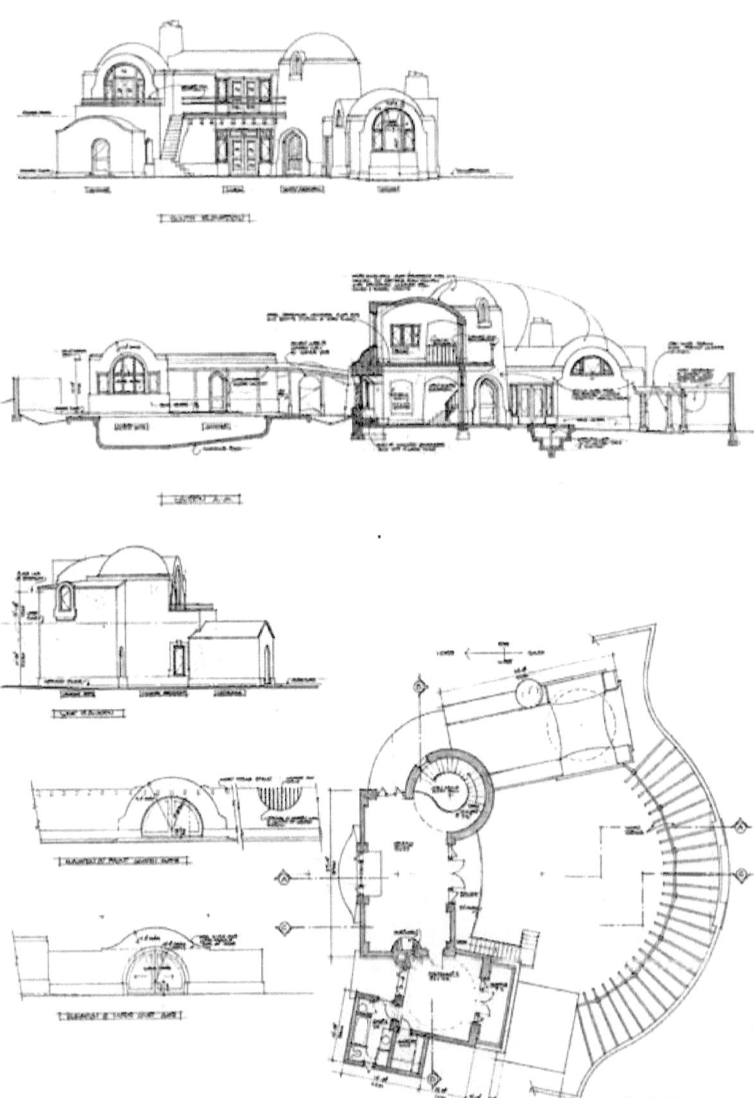

The style is reminiscent of Egyptian brick and stucco style by Ramses Wissa Wassaf.

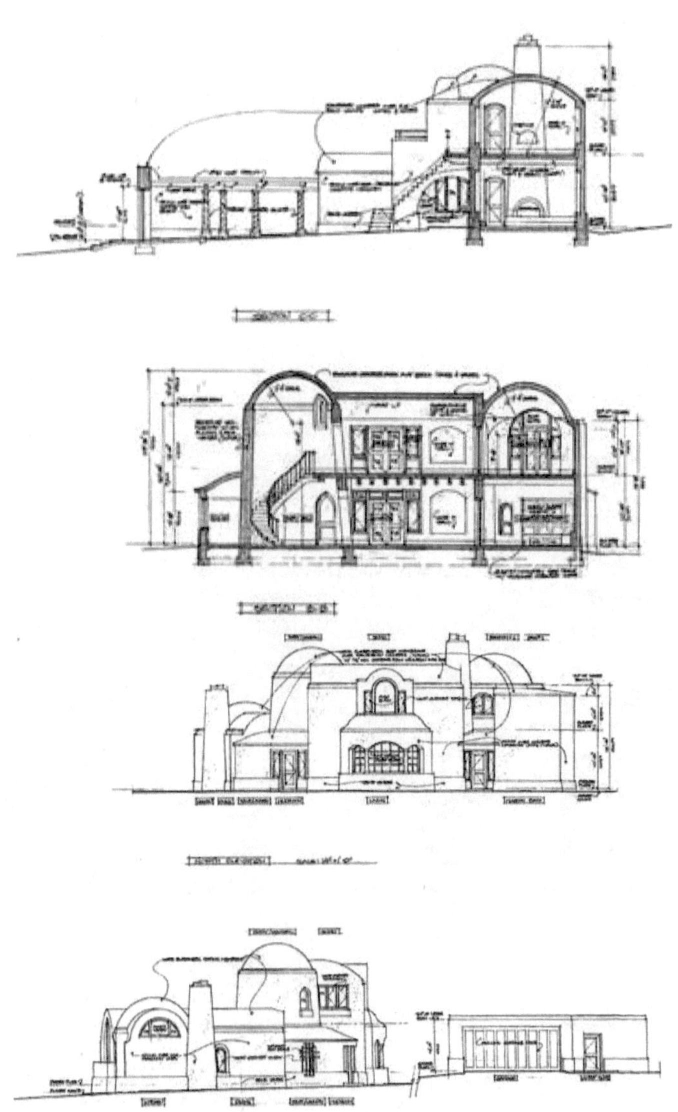

These Vaulted and domed roofs were commonly built with bricks from mud secured from along the flood plains of the Nile River. Today, these lovely complex forms are rendered in polystyrene foam by computer aided cutting machines. Individual elements are shop fabricated, labeled, shipped to the construction site by lightweight trailers, glued into place and covered, within and without, by cement plaster.

Chapter 7

Garage

Following the end of the Second World War, a blossoming middle class required new houses and this market was answered by Suburban Tract Development. The relatively humble tract house was inhabited by a mobile family and the automobile provided that mobility. In order to shelter the automobile from the elements and offer a covered access from the house to the car, an open sided, roofed "carport" was included as an attachment to the side of each house. As the family grew in numbers, so did the necessity for a second car become evident, with the resulting 2-car carport becoming standard tract house fare. Over time, houses became larger and larger, and the obvious next step was to enclose the 2-cars into a garage as an integral "room" within the overall house envelope.

The Garage provided security for the increasingly valuable automobiles plus allowed a modicum of effective heating for frigid climates that benefited starting the car in winter. The remotely actuated double garage door became a necessity for mom and a convenience for the whole family. The Double car garages were about eighteen feet square (6 square meters) with a single 16 foot (5 m) wide door. The door opened in an upward fashion to reside against the garage ceiling and tended to attempt to eat the car by slamming onto the car roof. The segmented garage door with automatic retraction solved that problem. "Better living through electronics" was the new marketing concept.

Since the American middle class were dedicated consumers, the garage soon performed another service. Most of the purchases that filled the shopping cart of the mall, within a week, landed in three places. These places were; in the trash can, under the kids' bed and, you guessed it … in the garage. The garage, by necessity, commenced to grow and grow. Then Dad decided that his familial well-being demanded that he become a do-it-yourself fanatic, thus one entire garage wall needed to be moved out to accommodate the "workshop." Needless to say, Dad never "did-it- himself" after the second week, but the long workbench was a perfect place to pile all those treasures flowing from Wal-Mart, Costco and Target.

Obviously with these pressures, the garage soon was to become by far the largest room in the entire house. The fact that the grandest space within the home was not even a living area, but rather a huge storage room for two objects that are, by design, perfectly capable of dwelling completely out of doors, does seem a bit odd. Not just odd, but decidedly absurd, in fact, but we do love our cars. To further this lunacy, it is, of course, necessary for the garage to be located at the front of the house to allow for street access. To digress a bit, the original garages in the 1920s were located off a small secondary road behind the property called an "alley." The Alley also was used to place trash cans and grass clippings for pickup by the city refuse crew. Often along these non-paved alleys the electrical, telephone and other wires, plus water and sewer lines were also located, thus mitigating the necessity of digging up the street and sidewalks every time a pipe

broke. Of course, these alleys took up quite a bit of the developers' land, so out they went in order to squeeze a few more postage stamp lots into the cash flow mix resulting in a better bottom line.

Now the small, narrow lots also have a "side yard setback" on each side of the lot and together with the huge garage, there was little "front" left for things like windows opening into living areas. Today, driving along nearly every subdivision street what one sees is a series of pathetic dwellings, hiding behind two items that are vying for attention, the mammoth "entry foyer" and the garage. You will also notice that there are two cars parked in front of the garage door. The garage is completely full of "stuff," so the cars are relegated to outside, now and forevermore. Duh?

Since this book is promoting smaller, more sensible houses you might well consider that it is possible to knock off 10-15 percent of the budget for your new house by eliminating the garage. This will work quite well unless your automobile is in the top ten of theft items or your location is in Point Barrow, Alaska. A good insurance policy and a crankcase oil heater will help wonders for those and four poles, a tarp, and some rope will easily put up some shade in Phoenix. Welcome to parking in the simple life.

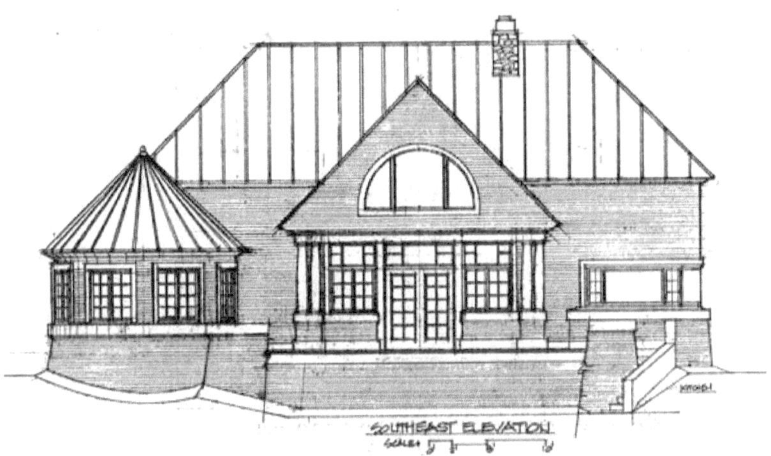

Classic Cottage

Classic Cottage and the following houses in this chapter all have attached garages and most contain two cars. Although the automobile is a major influence within the family, it has a service role and the attempt here is to downplay the garage within the overall visual aspect of the house. The garage has been attached opposite of the principal façade of Classic Cottage and the large roof hovers overhead to minimize attention toward the garage doors. The use of two single doors rather than a large double wide door reduces the scale while allowing the width of the garage to be increased. The garage in Classic Cottage allows access directly into the Foyer as well as a secondary access to the mud room/laundry and rear exit to the outdoors. With the addition of windows on the Northeast and Northwest walls, this garage could easily become a recreation room on occasions with sufficient space for billiards and table tennis.

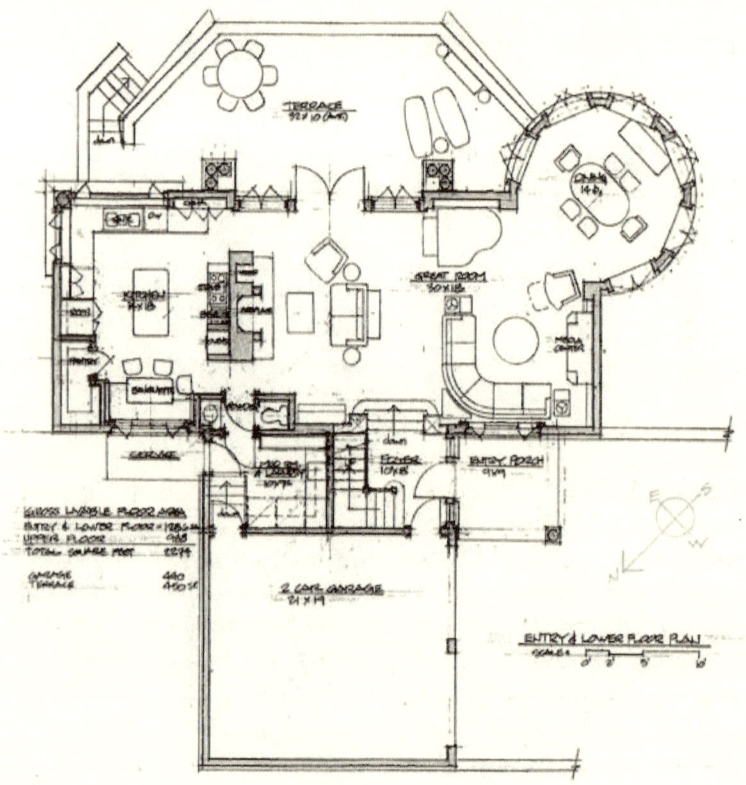

Classic Cottage – Floor Plan

Numerous versions of this basic floor plan are incorporated within the houses shown here. The free-flowing open plan linking Kitchen/Living/Dining into a continuous spatial sequence is the hallmark of the relaxed lifestyle of today. Each functional area is subtly defined by partial walls, bulging exteriors, and carefully placed groupings of furniture.

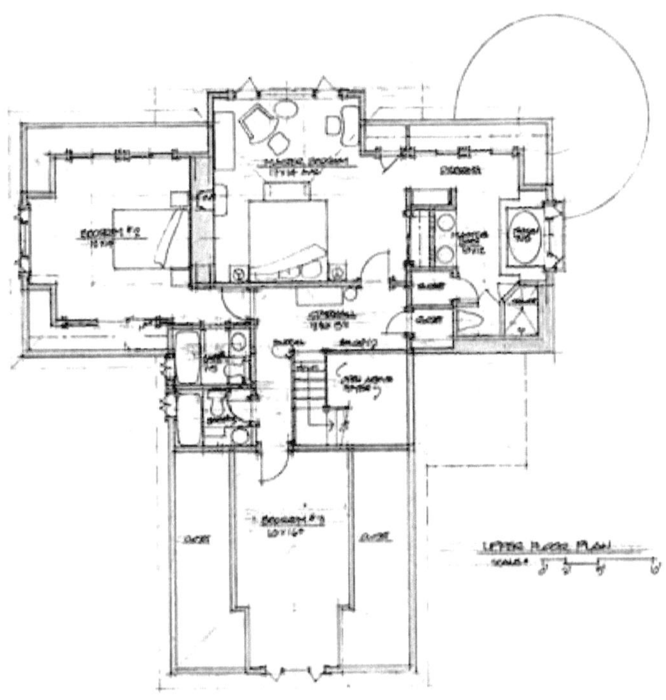

The upper floor of Classic Cottage is delineated by an encompassing roof that centers over each bedroom. The Master Suite enjoys a king-sized bed, fireplace, and sitting area facing a large arched window. The Master Bath has a roman tub, separate shower, double lavatories, plus ample dressing and closet space. The other two Bedrooms each have a private Bathroom, and large closets.

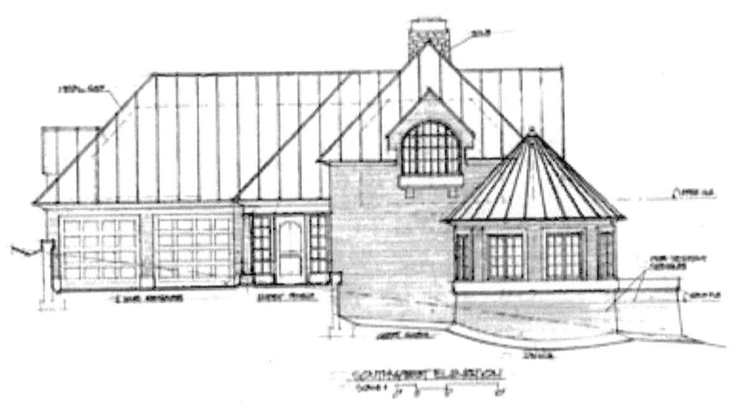

Chapter 8

Ornament

Adolph Hitler was a fascist that attempted to control the Politics of the World. He failed. Adolf Loos was a fascist that attempted to control the Architecture of the World. He succeeded. Adolf Loos was an Austrian Architect that, in 1908, put his ideas into print. Those literary beginnings were the spark that smoldered into fire and during the following century grew to a conflagration that consumed Architecture throughout the world. Loos authored Ornament and Crime where he turned the architectural philosophy of the previous five thousand years upside down.

From reviewing photographs of his built work, Loos was obviously intelligent but somewhat lacking as a creative designer. Early in his career, he was competing against supremely talented architects of the "secessionist" movement in Vienna, and "Art Noveau" in Paris and Brussels. Having been to the United States, he was intrigued by the emerging designs of the "Chicago school" tall buildings but, undoubtedly shamed by the towering talent and amazing drawing ability of Frank Lloyd Wright. Against this august competition, if he was going to become renown, Adolf needed a gimmick. The gimmick was to attack ornament. Loos wrote that the use of ornament was a "crime." He meant that literally.

Loos promulgated four defining tenets of his Architectural Dogma: 1. For the newly industrialized civilization, progress demands the elimination of ornament. 2. The built environment must reflect solely the technical simplicity (minimization) of the day. 3. All previous Architectural design styles of older eras are not "modern" and must be "eliminated." 4. The new Superior Cultural Status (1920s) demands that the only authentic architecture for the future is "modern" and must be based upon minimalist styles echoing industrial components.

Loos went on to say, "I have no need whatsoever to draw my designs. Good Architecture, how something is to be built, can be written. One can write the Parthenon." Since the Parthenon is the most sublimely beautiful of classical Greek buildings, Loos was not only an elitist, but he was also delusional as well. These delusions, however, were not lost on thousands of "modernist" architects that were to follow. Their shared delusions were the excuses for 90% of less talented multitudes of emerging architects to continue their process of denuding enrichment of Style from Architecture.

As the 21st century enfolds, together with computer aided design, the Loos ideal of "writing" architecture is mainstream. Architects not being able to draw from their innate creative wonder, only need to "click and paste" and thus ensure the continuance of the boring sameness of "modern architecture." How sad is this? But take heart Mom, your doilies on the armchair are safe. There is a new day dawning in Architecture and appreciation of the "old stuff" is rising again, and none too soon, thankfully.

Chapter 9

The Neighborhood

Villas A through J below are from a Neighborhood of small 52' X 75' (16m x23m) land parcels within a standard suburban subdivision. With limited lot area and the additional constraints of a two-car garage, floor space is organized to create maximum outside perimeter walls. Optimum use of windows is accommodated plus outside patio areas are defined when exterior walls are increased.

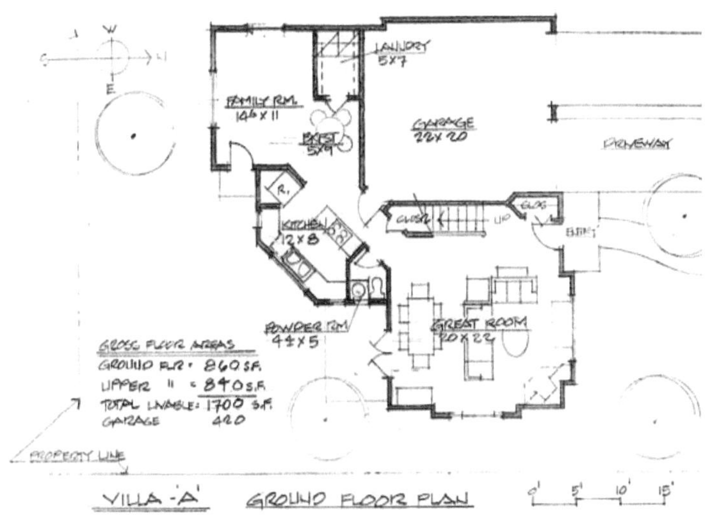

Note that the interior spaces that back up against the walls of the garage would not usually have windows in them. They are utility, closets, stair halls or other spaces that are open to and a part of other rooms. This plan literally wraps around the garage and the exterior wall undulates to encompass multiple expansive windows and glass doors. This effect allows two windows within every Bedroom for balanced light and natural ventilation. The second floor also has an upstairs terrace overlooking the private garden.

This terrace can be readily converted to an additional Study or Playroom. The house is complete in a livable floor area of 1,700 square feet (158 sq. meters).

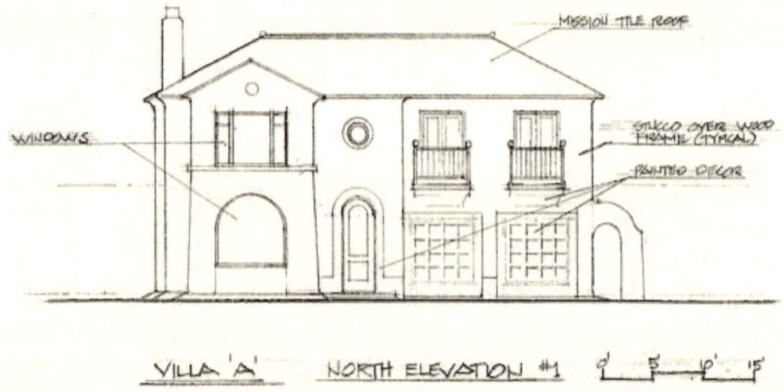

Two story plans are the most effective concept on small lots. The floor area at ground level is reduced allowing for greater exterior living space. The visual mass of the second floor also minimizes the attention toward the garages.

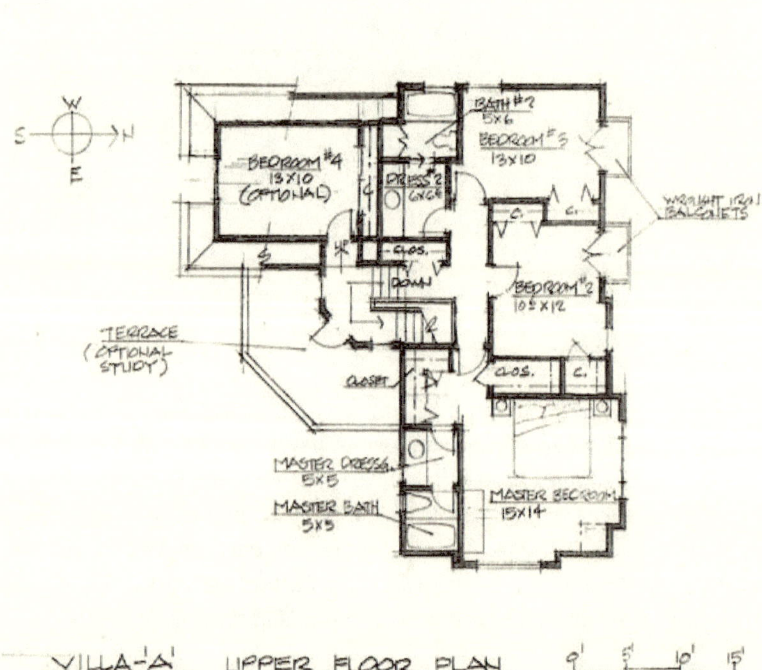

The street side North Elevation of Villa A shows three different Architectural styles affecting differing character while retaining the same floor plan layout. Elevation #1 utilizes a shortened roof overhang and Neo Santa Barbara Style, whereas the roof overhangs are extended in Elevation #2 resulting in a more Mediterranean feeling.

North Elevation #3 echoes the Santa Fe style with parapet roofs typical of arid climates of the western United States.

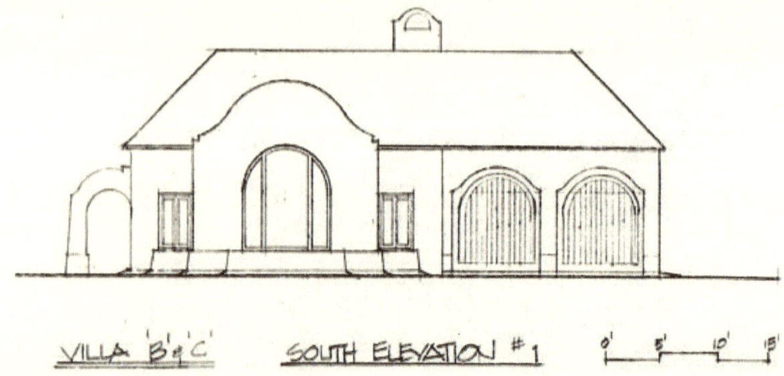

Villas B and C share the same three differing street elevations. South Elevation #1 evokes a mild Mission Style with a large arched picture window and two sidelites.

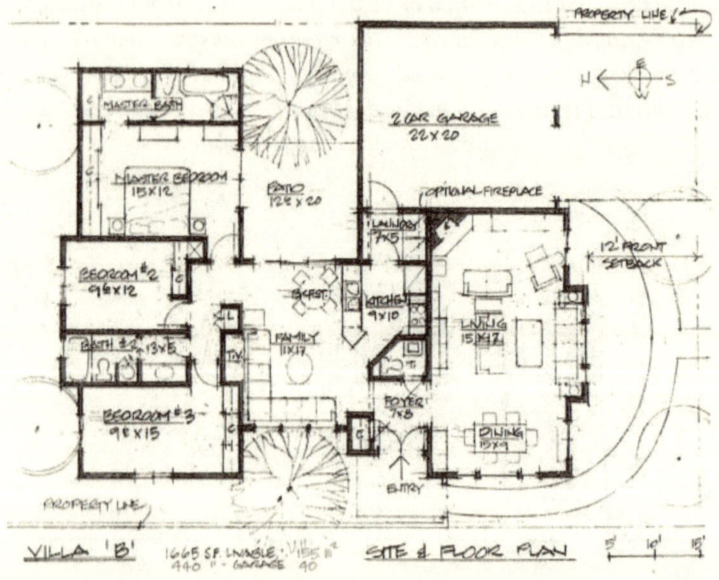

Villa B Floor Plan demonstrates how expanding the perimeter walls allows for maximum window area while creating protected courtyards. In this case, both exterior patios are around the corner from the street. Often builders complain that too much wall and too many corners increase the cost. If your builder echoes this sentiment, he is lazy. Fire him and get another. The Family Room is the functional link between Living/Dining and the Bedroom wing and offers a comfortable informal, bright gathering place.

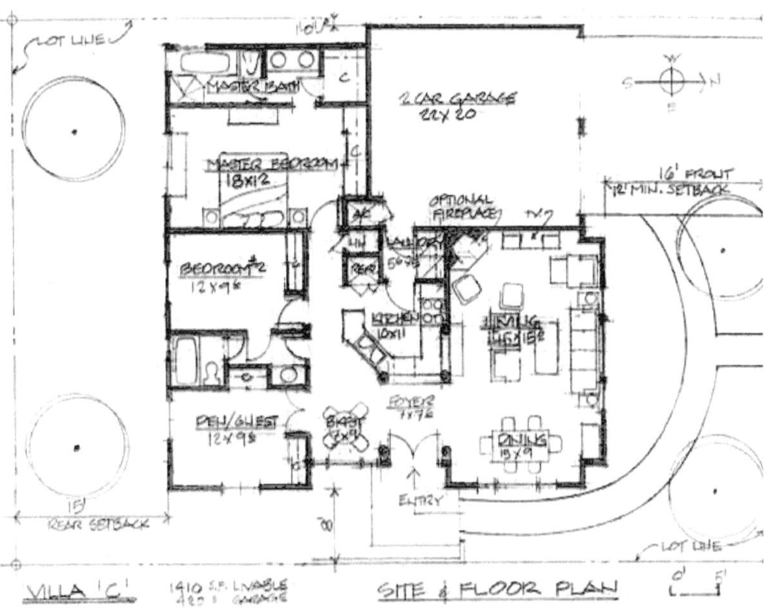

Villa C Floor Plan is smaller by 255 square feet (24 sq. meters) yet still retains the ample Living/Dining Room together with an open view from the Kitchen. Note that the furniture arrangements create cozy, defined conversational groupings.

Villa B and C South Elevation #2 is a conservative bit of French Country Style with the arched topped picture window added for a little spice.

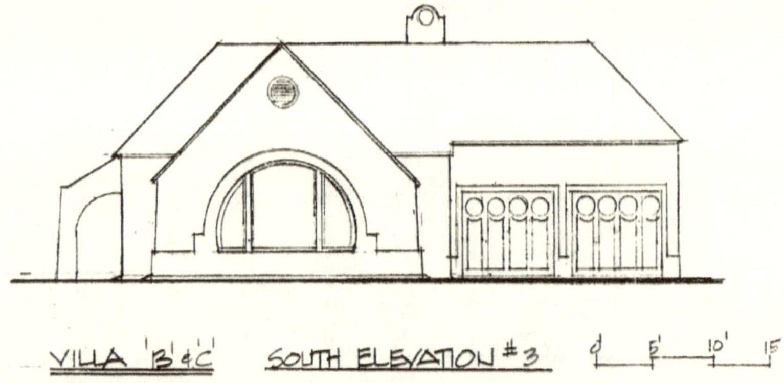

In South Elevation #3 above, the picture window has been significantly enlarged and the eave line has been lowered to add visual emphasis to the Living/Dining Room inside. Note that all these elevations may have the overhangs extended when being built in more rainy climates. Since the recommended overhang of 3 feet adds up to 20 percent of additional roof area, the elevations as shown are for cost savings.

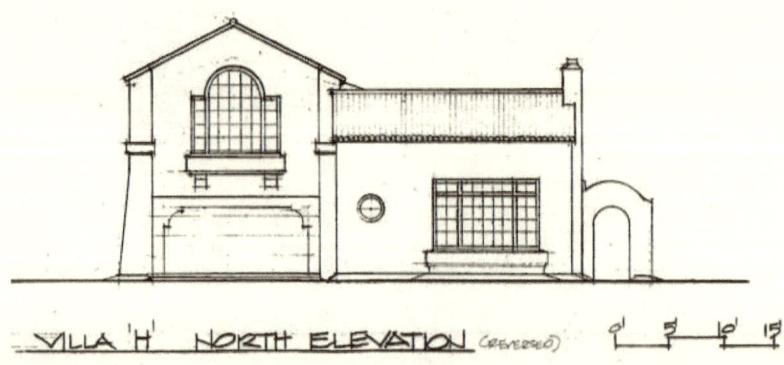

Villa H North Elevation shows how a significant second floor window above a garage can create a dramatic effect utilizing the garage door as a visual base for the façade

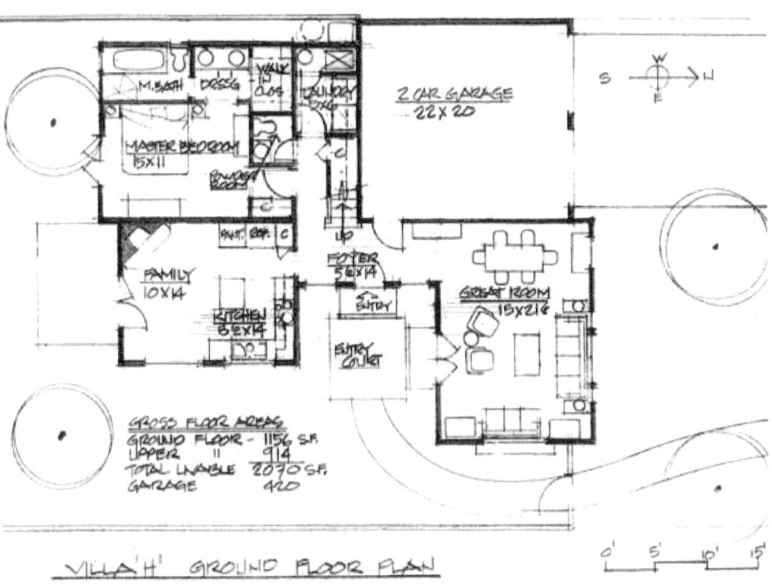

The Villa H Floor Plan once again utilizes a two-story concept to allow a larger floor area on a small site.

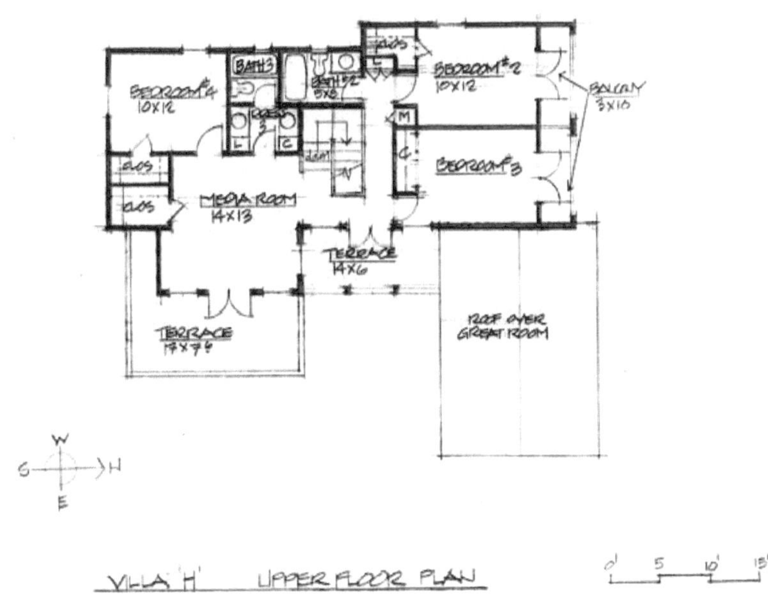

Villa H has multiple second floor terraces for outdoor living plus four bedrooms and three- and one-half baths. The total interior floor area is less than 2100 square feet (195 sq. meters).

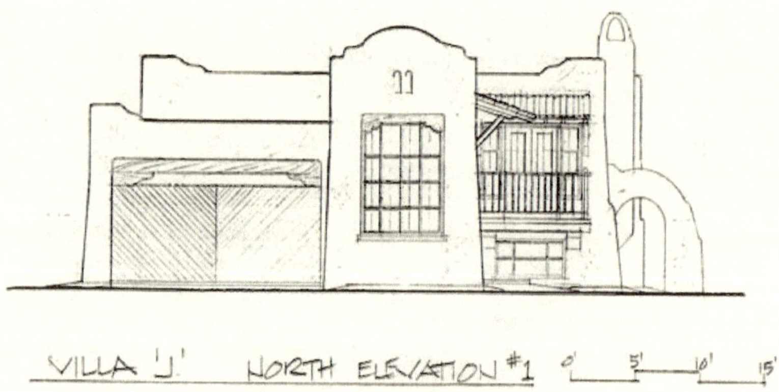

On occasion, a larger home is desired, but regulations do not allow a second story due to height restrictions. The solution here is to create a split-level plan where the lower floor is actually considered a basement, even though there are ample windows for all rooms.

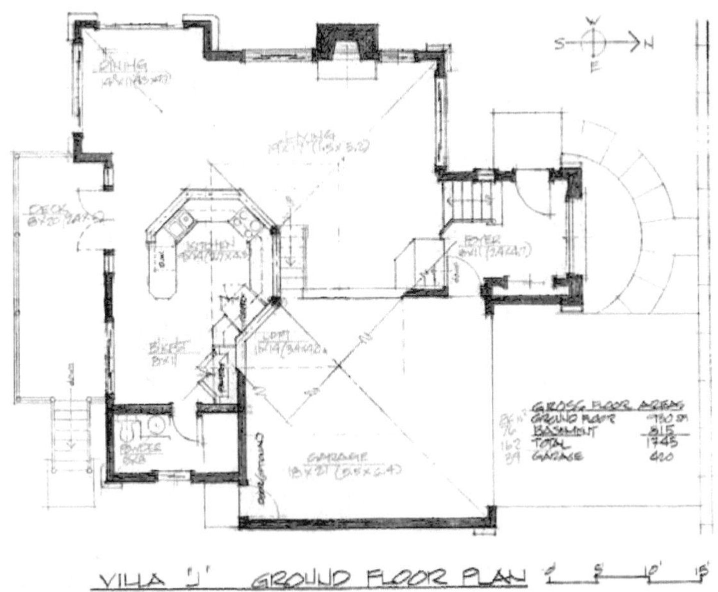

Here the Garage and Entry Foyer are on ground level and the upper floor living areas are raised a half level above. An optional Loft may be incorporated above a portion of the garage as shown in Elevation #2 design.

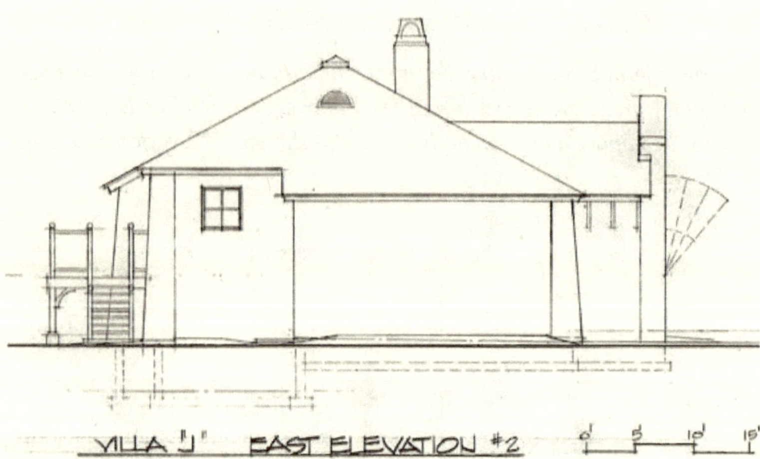

These Elevations demonstrate how the bulk of a two-story house can be effectively disguised to appear as a single-story building. This illusion could be enhanced through use of extended roof overhangs.

*The exterior raised deck provides additional living space adjacent to the
Kitchen and breakfast areas.*

*Villa J West Elevation #2 shows the ground level entrance door leading to the
integrated Foyer and interior stairway to both levels. An awning is drawn
with dashed lines to show an inexpensive way to shade a large sunny facing
window during a hot summer day. A pair of skylights is indicated on the top
of the hip roof. This allows a cascade of sunlight into the loft and down into
the living/Dining areas.*

Guesthouse over a Garage

Just in case you thought you would never see a garage with apartment combination.

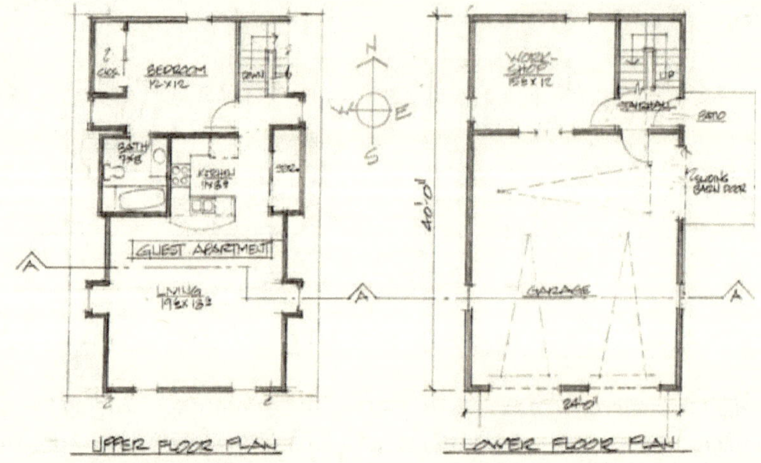

Here is a three car Garage with Workshop on the ground level and a tidy one-bedroom Guest Apartment above. The whole is disguised as a traditional Midwestern farm building with the living quarters nestled under a gambrel roof and a cupola with weathervane on top. There is a private entrance from the outside into the stair hall that accesses the apartment.

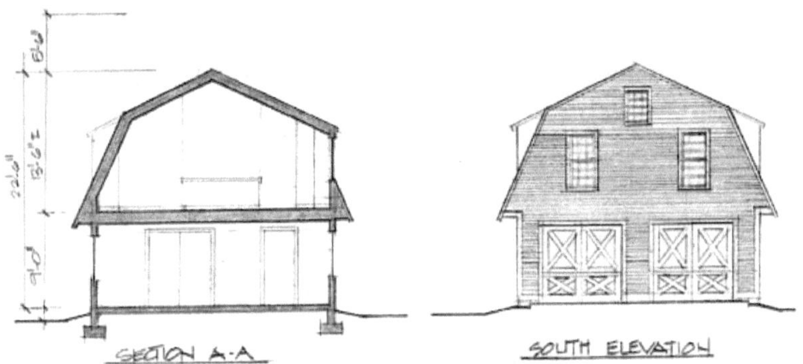

Ample light is introduced into the apartment through dormer windows on each side, and three windows on each end. The gambrel roof configuration allows for increased attic volume in the apartment. This is a throwback from the farmer's desire for an adequate hayloft.

Chapter 10

Entry Foyer

No self-respecting tract house in Middle America during the early 21st century was ever built without a special room dedicated to "arrival". This room is called the Foyer and serves to visually establish the first sense of coming to the home, impress the visitor, and to locate the cloak closet. A hundred years ago the foyer usually extended to become a hallway, often containing the stairs to upper floor rooms and was a "vestibule" serving as an airlock to prevent the cold or hot winds from entering the living areas of the house. Often there was a covered porch outside the entry door to the Foyer which served to shelter the arrivals prior to gaining entry plus allow a location for grandma's porch swing.

As the middle class became more affluent, the social requirement necessary to keep-up-with- the-Jones' mandated that the Porch and Foyer move together into a monstrous Lawyer Foyer. Ever increasing length and width was the order to accommodate the requisite 6' chandeliers hanging under the 20' ceiling. How very impressive! Of course, the porch swing disappeared along with grandma. The swing was relegated to a landfill, and grandma, first to a gated "seniors" community, and subsequently to "Nirvana land", of the Assisted Living Facility. There was no longer time enough to swing oneself and with her happy pills, grandma's swinging was outsourced for a measly three grand per month.

The revised house of the future will delete entirely the Foyer, save possible a return to a 4' x 5' vestibule including the cloak closet. This is only necessary in periods of drastic seasonal temperature change with families of more than 6 children, or both. With the Foyer incorporated within the overall living space through the "open plan concept," multi-use space is more efficiently allocated, and added windows can direct light, ventilation, and view into front facing rooms.

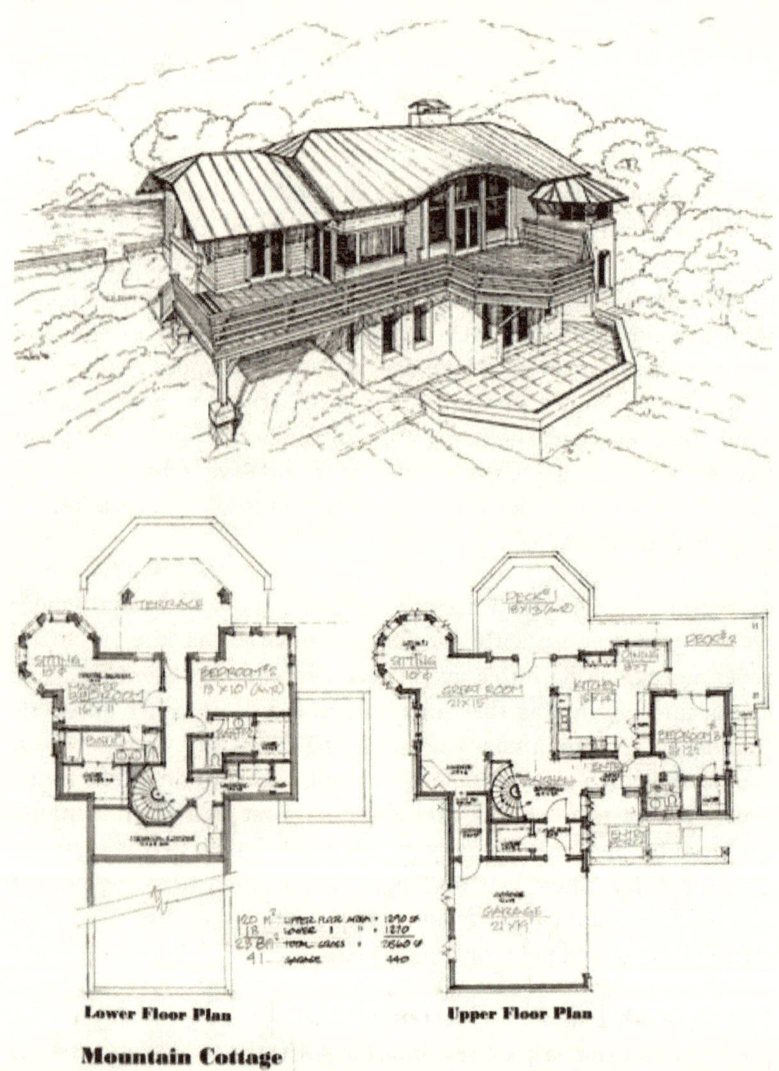

Mountain Cottage

The entry foyer within Mountain Cottage is tiny, yet allows immediate access to Kitchen, Bedroom #3, and the Stair Hall. A separate vestibule separates the Garage from the Stair Hall.

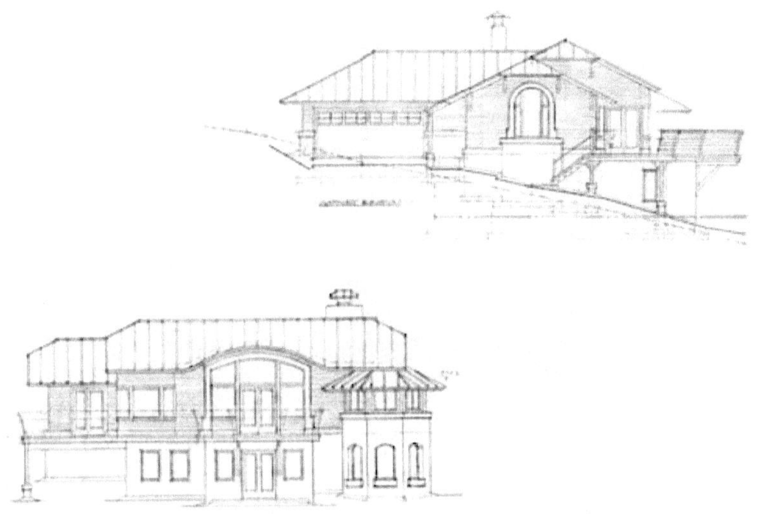

An entire lower floor is tucked into the hillside yet opens to a covered terrace.

Chapter 11

Living Room

In 1890, the Living Room was called the "Parlor" and nobody lived there. Not only that, the family, children, and especially the pets were not even allowed to go into the Parlor because they might track mud on the rug, soil the armchair's doilies, or cause dust to settle onto the piano bench. The Parlor was reserved for "guests" and was the "showcase" room of the house. This was not a problem for the kids. They played outside where they could spread mud and mayhem at will. Bereft of cell phones, computers, television, exercise machines, Fuse-ball, Xboxes, the children used their imaginations while being as far away as possible from the house so, mom could not find them and forced them to do "chores".

As the twentieth century haltingly emerged toward its second decade, fewer families were utilizing household servants. Since compartmented and segregated spaces were less required for privacy, the "open plan concept" took hold and Living (Parlor), Dining and Kitchen frequently became a single continuous space. Lifestyle at home was also increasingly less formal and the new more relaxed, family condition welcomed the focuses of new social generators, the telephone, radio, then television and ultimately the home computer. In the 1950's, television came to occupy the primary focus within The Living Room and the Parlor disappeared in name and function. Thanks to TV, the Living Room commenced to live up to its name. Within open planning, Mom could view the TV from the kitchen and never miss an episode of her favorite "Soap".

Even as the old wood stove disappeared from the kitchen, the fireplace in the living room remained as a visual icon and often it still burned real wood. It was no longer needed since central air- conditioning with an automatic control system took the chill off, yet the fireplace added "charm" and "coziness" to the living room. Charm was important to Mom, although Dad had no clue what that meant. Take a look at any office building erected within the last ninety years to prove this point. To men, charm was a kind of bracelet that his prepubescent daughter wore. Since most Architects are, and were, men, contemporary house design generally missed the boat when charm left the dock. Do not even mention "cozy." Four generations of architects have spread their boring yet "Modern" ilk within suburbia and managed to infect nearly a quarter of single-family houses, to say nothing of virtually all multi-family dwellings. I digress, however.

Modernist designed living rooms still often retain a fireplace, albeit with gas fired logs, and touch-of-a-button igniters. It may be fortunate if they do not burn wood, since most architects today have never heard of Benjamin Thompson (no, not Ben Franklin). Thompson, or more formally recognized as Count Rumford, promulgated the workable physics for non-smoking and efficient fireplaces over two hundred years ago. That is science, but as "art", contemporary designers have relegated the fireplace to a small hole at the bottom of a huge wall with no sense of character of feeling or warmth.

By the 1990's, the Living Room once again became a parlor when it was wedged against the Foyer and wall of the garage with only a single window facing front. Alone and forlorn, the "Living" part of its use was now entrusted to the "Family Room", where the 52" wide screen HDTV is now located, and the piano now collects dust in the new Parlor.

Coziness will return as houses continue to decrease in size during the next two decades. The Living Room and Family Room will become one. A fireplace, TV, and possibly even the piano will share the same area. Without the attached garage, there will be more window space for balanced natural lighting. With reduced ceiling heights, air conditioning and heating will be less costly. Tomorrow's spaces will be less huge, but decidedly more conducive of the basic activity within the Living room.

Mountain Villa, to be fair, is not really a little house as it was originally intended to be a Bed and Breakfast lodge. It does, however, exhibit how a relatively spacious Living/Dining/Kitchen "Great Room" can also have a cozy feeling within the various sitting areas. There are covered terraces on both ends of the Great Room and an additional balcony facing the downhill view.

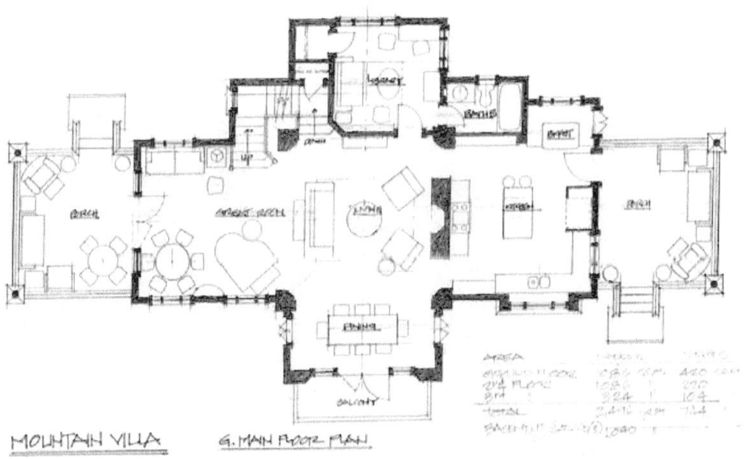

The total floor area including all four levels is 3536 square feet (327 sq. meters) which includes a large single car garage. There are a total of five Bedrooms including the Library/Guest Room and five full Bathrooms.

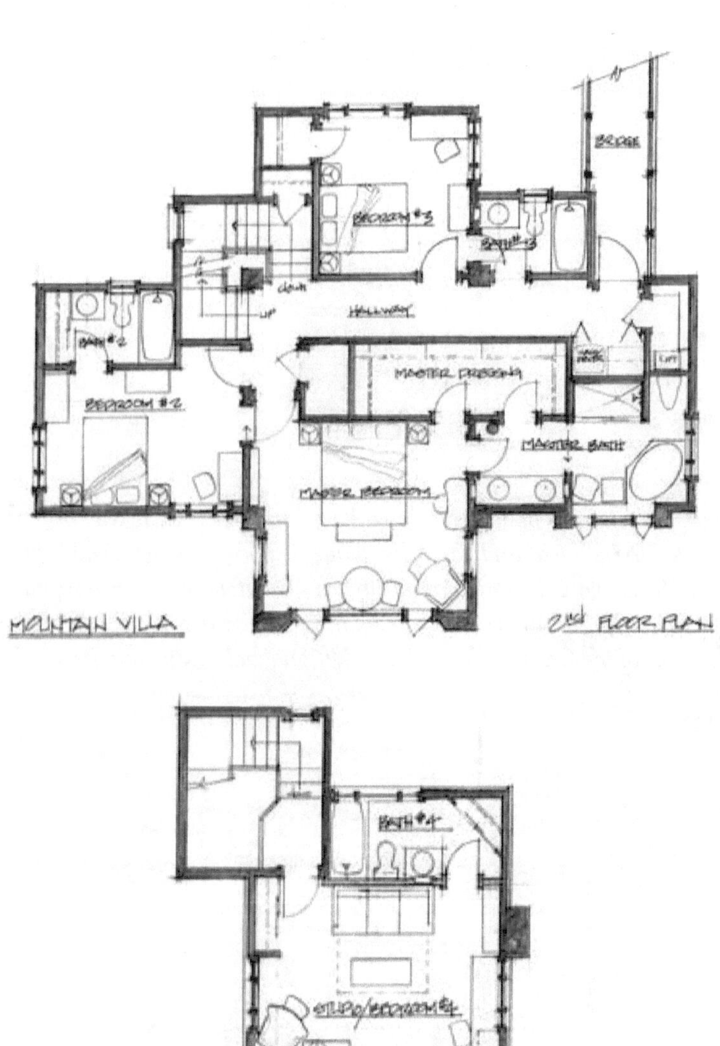

The fourth floor does double duty as a studio and retreat for those with healthy legs. The Terrace affords a splendid view when located in a proper setting.

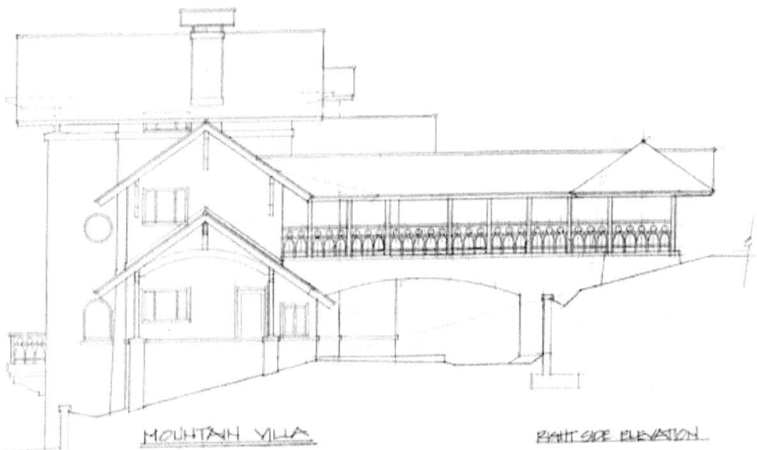

The above elevation shows the method of integrating the building into the sloping site. The covered bridge allows access to the second-floor level and is an additional fire escape from this and the floor above.

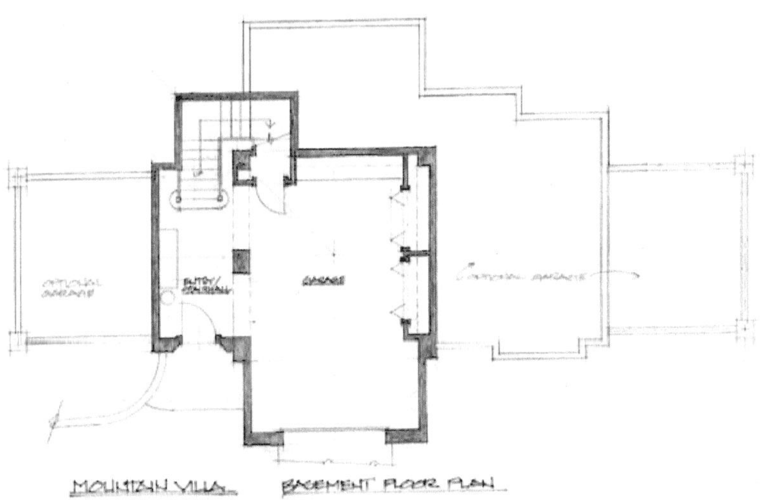

The Basement Floor is a walkout to the lowest ground level and serves as the vehicular drop-off point and access to the Garage. Additionally, three cars can easily be added in the Bed and Breakfast mode.

The Uphill Elevation opens off a courtyard with direct access to the library and to both covered Terraces at each end of the building.

Chapter 12

Pro Bono

In ancient Latin, the phrase "Pro Bono" means for the good. In current terms, the good is extended to those who benefit, and it is without compensation. Since creating one's home is usually the greatest investment that people undertake, any "pro bono" to save costs is most welcome. Good luck.

The single most expensive portion of creating a house in today's world has nothing to do with building the structure. The expense is, of course, the amount of interest and fees necessary to borrow the money to pay for it. Over the course of a typical thirty-year mortgage, the homeowner will pay for the house numerous times over, depending upon the rate of interest. The illusion is shared that "Home Equity" will grow over time resulting in an accrual of savings. Thanks to recent "bankster" chicanery in the mortgage marker, in actual fact, the homeowner is really only renting the house. All those years of paying the bank were a gift to the bank, since most real equity has been lost after the bubble burst. The lucky homeowner just lost value; many have been foreclosed upon and lost the house.

But I want to own my own home, you say. Is there a solution to this dilemma?

Two thoughts come to mind, a Little Patience and a Little House. Many cultures throughout the world have the curious custom of saving in order to purchase and are willing to either wait to commence building or build incrementally whenever partial funds are available. Typically, these people build much smaller dwellings for obvious reasons. Less "civilized" cultures often utilize local indigenous building materials and help their neighbors with the actual construction as a shared Pro Bono system. A concept of Caring and Sharing may seem odd to contemporary mindsets, but the Amish have been doing it for more than a century and adaptation to a similar method would not necessarily require a change in either religion or dress code.

On rare occasions, governments actually undertake programs to assist homeownership. Decades ago, the government of Cost Rica responded to the lack of ability for the poor to obtain adequate housing by instituting the Bono de la Vivienda which was a Mortgage (market) plan at a minimum interest rate. When the people were having difficulty paying the principal and interest, the government converted the program to a housing grant system and now many can live in a dignified small house of their own.

With the Costa Rican ideals, a series of house designs as follows, are shown which are offered to add bold, dignity and grace to little houses. Welcome to Pro Bono.

On the opposite extreme is Tica Cottage. A half century ago, when emerging families in Costa Rica needed small mortgage amounts to build a house, the Government instituted a program called the "Bono de la Vivienda" (Housing Bond) Elevation 'A' above is intended to be constructed with foundation, floors, walls and roof totally of polystyrene foam covered with fiberglass lath and cement plaster. A little house like this can be prefabricated, erected in two days, completed in another month and the family moved in with happy smiles on their faces a couple of days later.

TICA COTTAGE FRONT ELEVATION B

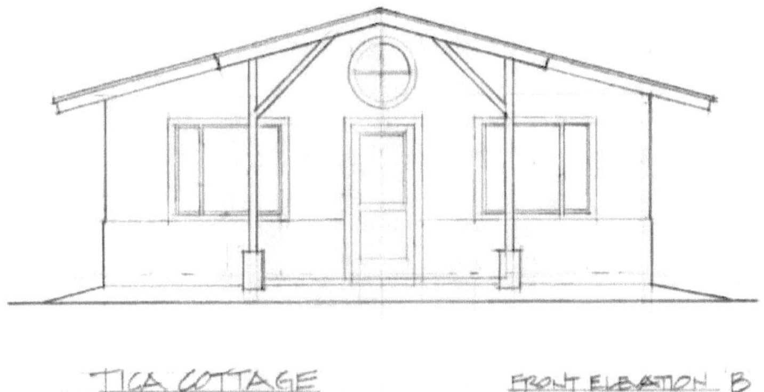

Here are two versions of the same small Bono house. Front Elevation 'B' is typical of thousands of little panelized concrete walled buildings with either a steel or wood framed roof. The walls are plastered inside and out then painted, usually off-white with a blue wainscot around the outside perimeter.

TICA COTTAGE FLOOR PLAN

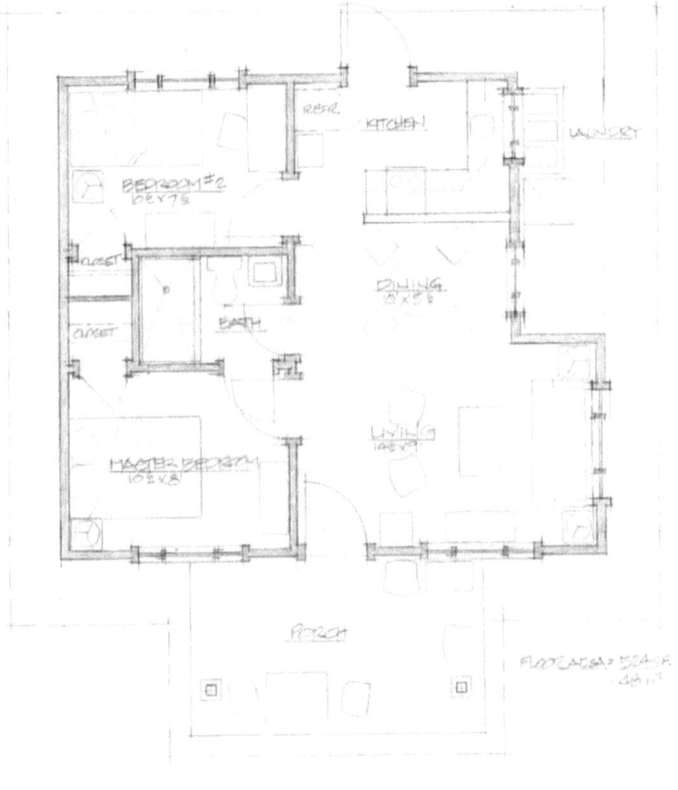

The maximum size to qualify for the Bono Plan in Costa Rica is 524 square feet (48 sq. meters) interior livable floor area as shown here. Living and Dining areas share the same space and the optional wall separating the Kitchen may be lowered to counter height for more informality. A Front Porch is a must for rainy climates. Generous overhangs allow for walking around the perimeter of the house and typically a 2' wide extended walkway surrounds the house. The laundry sink and washing machine are outside and the roof overhang allows sufficient space for air drying the clothes.

Elocuencia Cottage

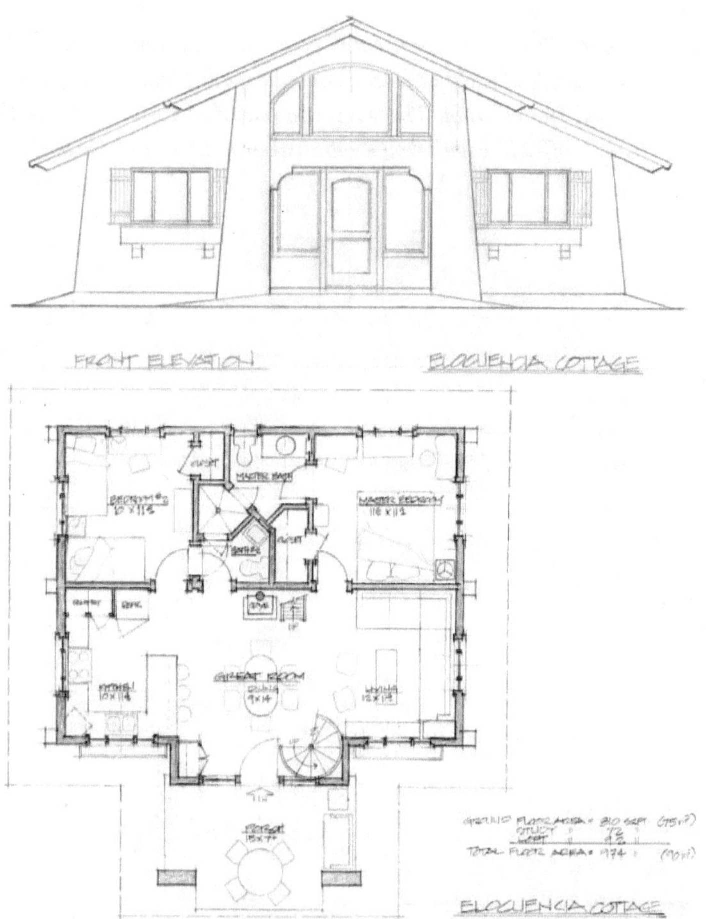

This cottage is a variation on the theme established within Tica Cottage above. There is, however, a twist.

Beneath the gently sloping roof, lie two additional cozy areas that are tucked up under the14' (4.3 m) high ridge line above the Bathroom and covered porch. A ships ladder adjacent to the fireplace ascends to a loft just large enough for a couple of single beds and a small desk. With a grand window, the other loft is the perfect place for a cozy study and access is from a space saving circular stairway. Both lofts utilize room volume that is normally not used other than open space plus there can be additional storage (accessed from the loft) above either Bedroom if lowered ceilings are used.

A careful look at both the Kitchen and Bathroom layouts will demonstrate how small spaces can be both efficient and pleasing to use. The "Great Room" concept links visually the entire Kitchen/Dining/Living areas as well as the two lofts. Both Bedrooms have Bathrooms that share a common shower stall. The closet in the Master Bedroom can accommodate a piggy-back washer/dryer.

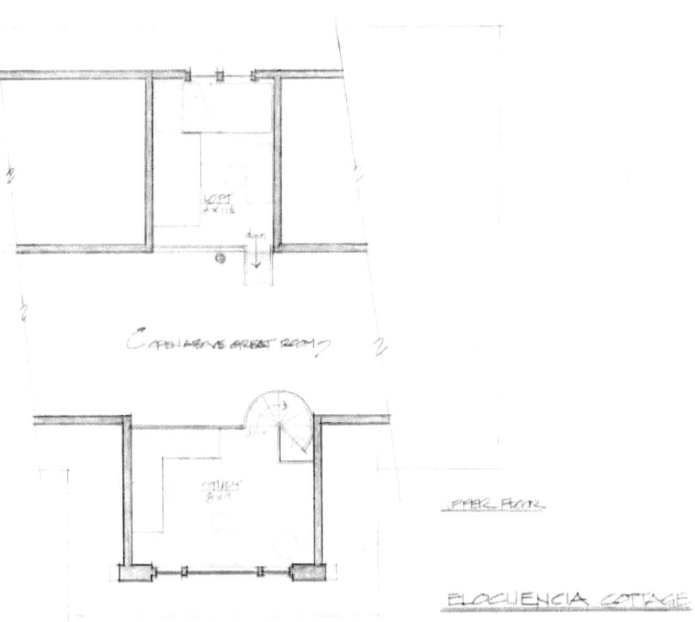

With a total floor area less than a thousand square feet (90 sq. meters), this cottage enjoys an efficient and comfortable plan while presenting a dignified face to all.

Alta Chalet

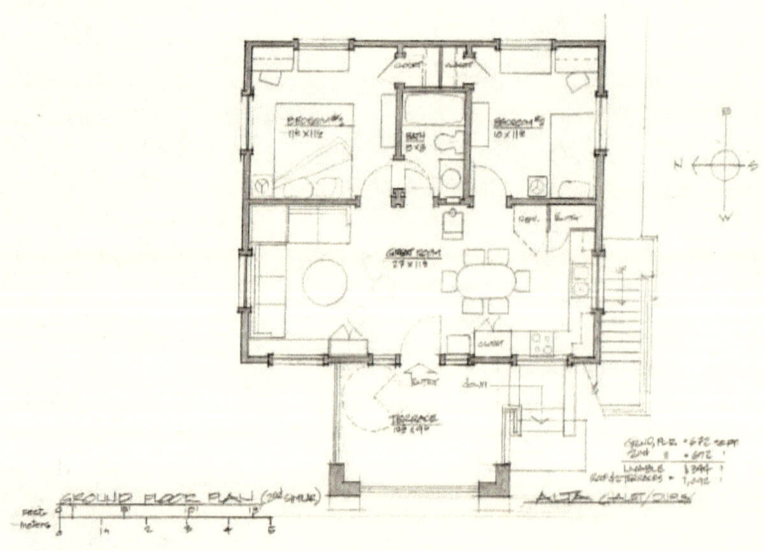

Alta Chalet is 672 square feet (63 sq meters) in livable floor area but also enjoys the option of an upper-level loft area accessed from a spiral stairway on the front terrace.

Alta Duplex

With an exterior stairway up to the front terrace, Alta Chalet becomes Alta Duplex. Both floor plans are the same and an optional spiral stairway extends from the upper front terrace to a rooftop deck covering the entire building. Utilizing a greenhouse roof system, this entire rooftop can function as a garden for growing fruits, vegetables and flowers.

The tiny building footprint will easily fit within a 40' (12m) square exclusive of automobile parking. This will enable a density of up to 40 dwellings per acre within a pedestrian accessed site configuration or 20 per acre with vehicular parking.

Dale's House

Sometimes, within multi-family zoning classifications it is permissible by the "City" to allow a third-floor level to a single-family house. In the case of Dale's House an artist's studio was added resulting in a superb hideaway. Of course, the government makes certain that the owner does not rent out the studio to someone other than a family member.

This house also has a small footprint and since the double car garage is within the building, this house can fit on a 50X50 foot (15X15 meter) square lot. This size is subject to zoning setback requirements.

The total livable floor area is 1596 square feet (148 sq. meters) plus the Garage with laundry/storage at 504 sq. ft. (47 sq. m).

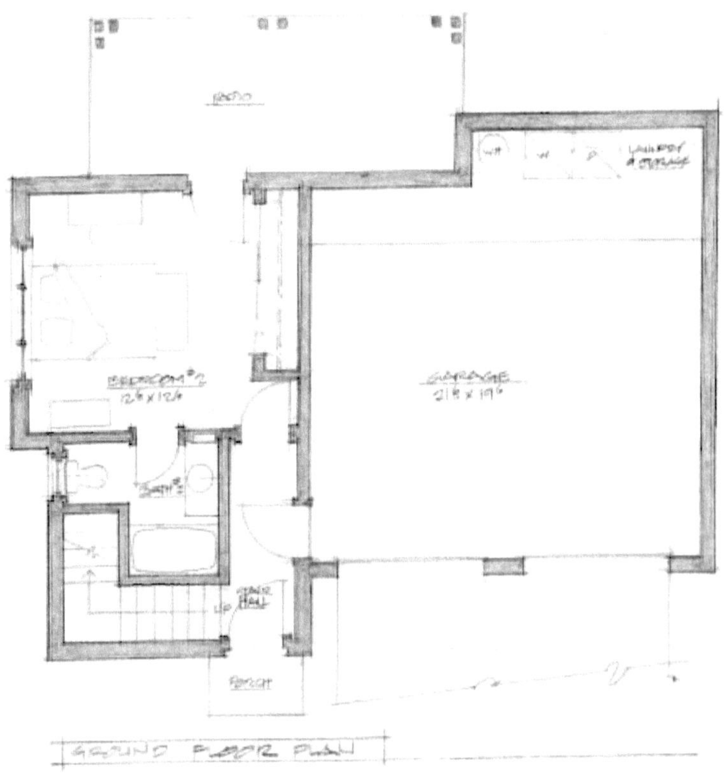

The vestibule and stair hall leads immediately up to the Living areas above. Bedroom #2 opens to a covered patio. The double car garage contains a laundry area.

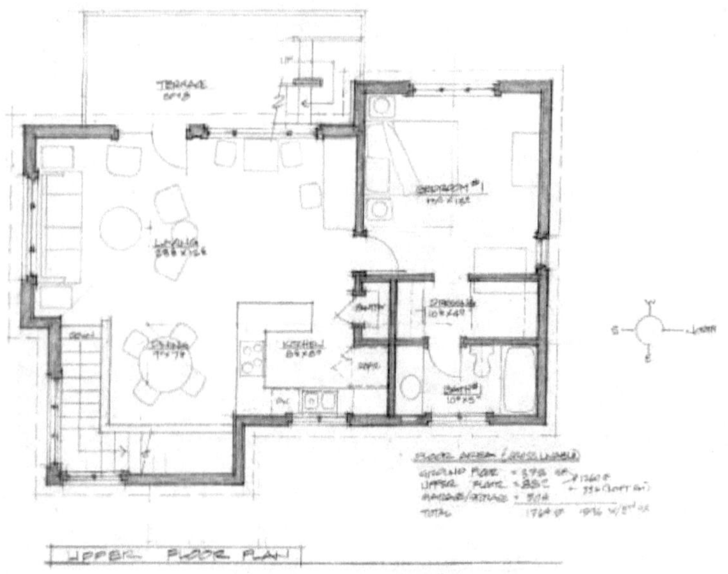

The open plan Great Room looks to a terrace with staircase up to the Loft above.

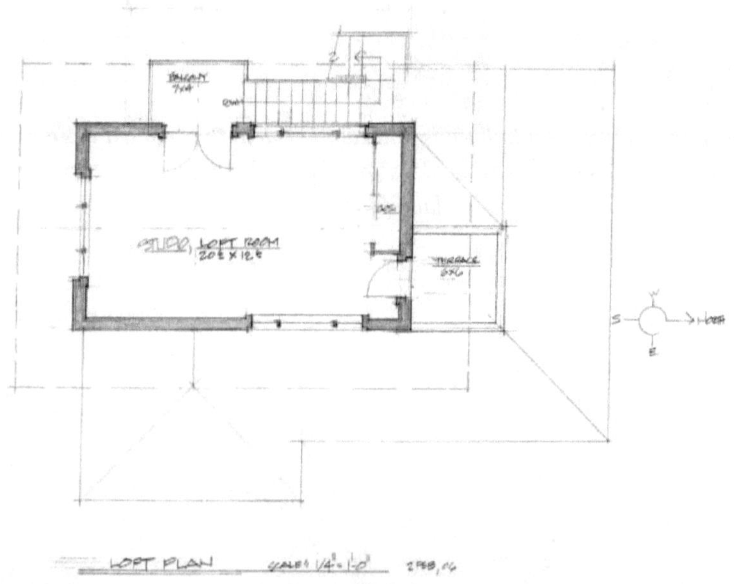

The Studio Loft can be utilized as a bedroom by converting the small terrace to a bathroom.

EAST ELEVATION

Chapter 13

Style

Contemporary Architects do not like the word "style." To them, style connotes decadence and frivolity from the past. I beg to differ. Style relates to character and qualifies a design with regard to the emotional aspects of a house. All buildings have style, it is just that much of modern or contemporary style is emotionless, banal, and quite frankly, ugly.

In 1929, an exposition in Barcelona, Spain ushered in a new era of architectural dogma. Mies Van der Rohe designed a particularly poetic pavilion in the new Modern style which was a collection of simple horizontal and vertical planes and not much else. This was the very first noted example of "boxitecture." Along with a desire to create componentized buildings, this new philosophy, that a "House is a machine for living in," was embraced by the entirety of four generations of Architects and led them all down a path toward boring sameness.

A hundred years ago, a fledgling Architect, to become successful, required a modicum of something called "talent." With the new modernism as professed via Ivy League university regimen, any minimalist brained bean counter that could draw straight lines was sanctified as a "contemporary" Architect. The planet continues to suffer from this ilk, especially as related to houses.

Even the Modernist's claim to founding the concept of pre-engineered, prefabricated, componentized building systems was a farce. Seventy-eight years before that pavilion in Barcelona, there was another exposition pavilion called The Crystal Palace in London, which was actually one of the world's first major componentized structures. This Building covered more than 17 acres under roof, was a huge greenhouse 70 feet tall and was conceptualized, designed, fabricated of component parts, erected, and the exhibits installed within nine months. Being a decidedly beautiful glass building, it was anything but "minimalist" in style.

The modernists seized upon a truly worthy by-line stating that "form follows function." They then continued to encapsulate every possible function into an oversized three-dimensional shipping crate as if people were actually apples or oranges. An additional edict of the modernist movement still professes that 'less is more." That may sometimes have relevance to things other than talent, but common sense may question the results of their contemporary efforts. Do not be misled, less is still less.

A couple of decades ago, a few Architects finally became bored with Boxitecture and decided to branch out into a few other directions. Not being content to read a bit of history for inspiration, they threw all the past away and commenced to do something "completely different." Had they studied their history, they would have realized that most elements of style had actually

been demonstrated. They also would have realized that most of the BEAUTY in Architecture had been built, refined, and built repeatedly throughout previous generations.

Since the truly talented were already employed by the film industry, these "archicontexturalists" commenced to express what solely remained within their palates, namely UGLY. Not only did they do their utmost best to demonstrate ugly, but they also deemed to include every possible ugly they could incorporate into every single building all at once. This style has evolved into the new order of Shockitecture {together with first cousin Narcissitecture) and is usually found most prevalent in the design of Art Museums. It seems that Contemporary Art and the Shockitecture Style have an incestuous symbiotic relationship wherein the genetic encoding falls somewhere between Whaaaat? And Why?

Thankfully, for most small residential buildings, Shockitecture is all too expensive and is of insufficient ego-gratification for the archicontexturalists to bother with. Mom will be grateful. Suffice to say, Style is a personal thing and the visual character of a house, both inside and out, needs to address practical functions and emotional issues as well. There really is no correct style for little houses of the future. If the Architect and associated builder complete a building that keeps the rain out and does not fall down, any style is fine. But remember, Mom is watching.

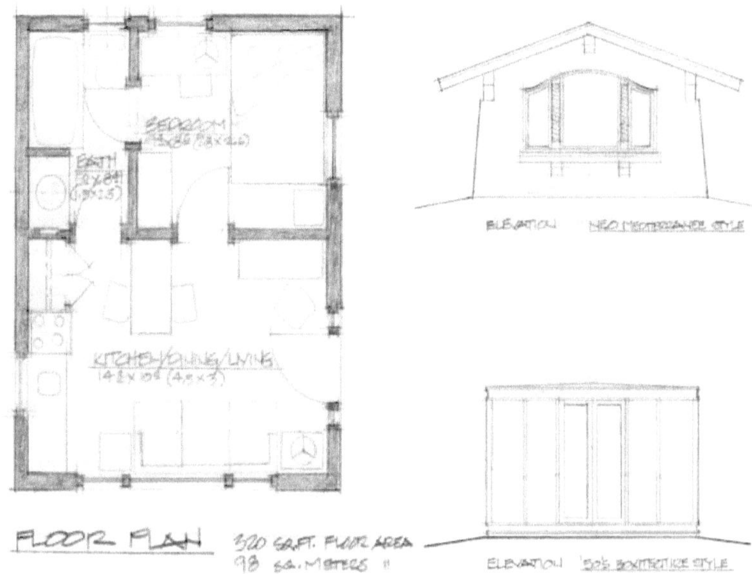

The Smallest House

Yes, this is the smallest house in the book. That being so, it also is an excellent venue to demonstrate a few comparisons between different Architectural Styles. After reading the rant earlier in this chapter, it is only fair for you to evaluate for yourselves the relative merits of a few alternative design styles as shown on the front elevation of this same building.

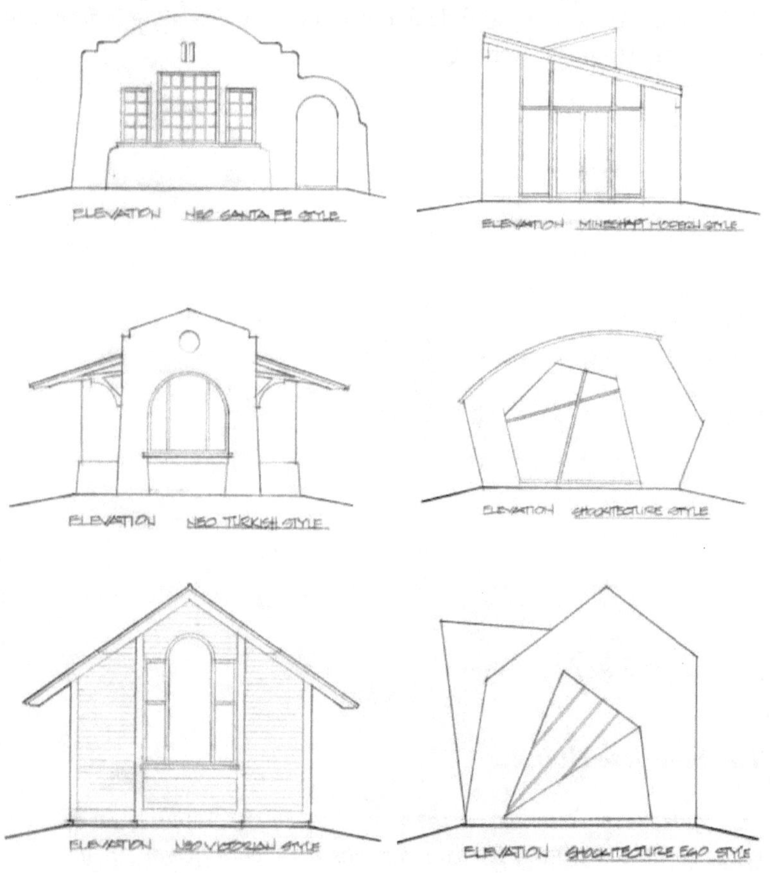

So here are eight examples for your review. It would not have been difficult to do a dozen or more, since there are literally thousands of "styles" available to a sufficiently talented designer. Why are the vast majority of Architect designed houses limited to Boxitecture and Shockitecture styles? Hmmm. That is a good question.

Chapter 14

Kitchen

"Home is where the hearth is." Okay, so what is a hearth? Even before the Neanderthal homemaker moved out of the cave, there was a fire to keep warm and cook the latest Mastodon delicacy. Immediately in front of the fire was a warm spot on the ground. This was the "hearth." Throughout the subsequent living environment, the hearth evolved into a room call the Kitchen, and even within the bowels of great mansions of the aristocracy, this place was always the soul of the home. Of course, the aristocrats hardly went there, but who cared, the servants did, and the working class does deserve a few perks.

By the early 1950s the middle class had emerged and the only residual servant still working in the kitchen was called Mom. The old wood stove had long departed to be replaced with the latest gas or electric "range" and sometimes the range was split into two pieces referred to as the "cooktop" and the "double ovens." Grandma's icebox had morphed into a double wide "refrigerator" which even had a hatch in the door that spit out ice, and cold water. The washtub on the counter evolved into a two compartment "drop-in sink" with hot and cold running water. Under a drain hole of one of the sinks now resided a "disposal unit" which at the flip of a switch all of the leftover garbage was instantly ground to smithereens and flushed away. The double sinks were actually not needed for washing the dishes anymore since Mom now had a "dishwasher." No, this was not one of the children forced into KP duty. The dishwasher was invented by an upper-class lady in Chicago a hundred years ago who was sick and tired of having the crystal stemware become expensive shards due to a series of clumsy maids. This ingenious lady observed that if dishes were subjected to 175° F water being sprayed on them, all the food would just slide off and sparkling wine glasses would emerge. She designed and perfected the machine to do just this, took in a male business partner (nobody believed a woman could be an industrialist!) and proceeded to establish a company called Hobart which today we recognize as a first-class home appliance called Kitchen Aid. The major appliances soon were offered in lovely color co-ordinate hues with Mom able to choose from" harvest gold" "turquoise", "avocado green" "appliance white", and ultimately "stainless steel."

Not to be outdone, a defense contractor that was playing with microwave energy discovered that these invisible waves of the electromagnetic spectrum were capable of cooking anything composed partially of water. And they cooked them really fast. What used to take an hour could be blasted in the "microwave oven" and there, mere seconds later, your instant meal was ready to squat and gobble.

Wow! With all these time savers, Mom could have more leisure hours for discussing menus with the neighbor and watching Julia Child baking croissants. Well, not quite. Mom had to get a job. Paying for that kitchen and the remainder of their suburban American Dream home has proved to be a never-ending daunting task, even for a two-wage earner family. Not to worry though. You see, Mom doesn't really use that wonderful show kitchen with its Tuscany Style arched hood oven, the massive "commercial grade" range. The "island" center with spacious wine rack and four

adjacent bar stools are sitting empty and forlorn. The near acres of polished granite countertop over the double "warming drawers" are abandoned, to say nothing of the aforementioned necessities. Nowadays most moms just pick up the frozen "package" cuisines, stick'em into the microwave, nuke'em and serve.

Moving into decade number two of the 21st Century, if you are still able to keep up with the mortgage, Mom's "show" kitchen may now come into its own. Mom, and maybe even the kids, can experience a delightful few minutes of time in the kitchen while beginning to rediscover the joys waiting there. Preparing and cooking food, to say nothing of growing a kitchen garden, allows us to focus our attention upon one of the basic activities that sustains the family. It is doubly rewarding. Not only is it creative fun, but also eating is the most enjoyable simple pleasure that occurs within the home. Well, maybe eating while watching television is actually the most enjoyable.

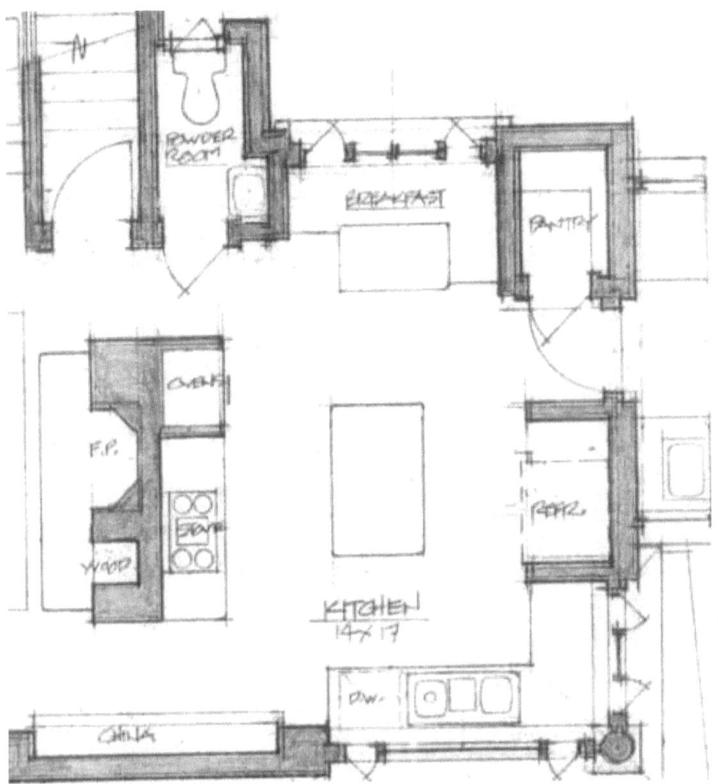

Cynthia's Manor has a kitchen that even a professional chef could love. Although larger than what one would expect within a small house, it is a true living space for the soul of a house. Ample space for two persons to work in, there is a breakfast nook for three other "kibitzers" to enjoy the business at hand without being in harm's way of the chopping knife.

Chapter 15

Kitchen Planning & Design

The wave of the future in housing will likely portend smaller and more cozy as primary attributes. Kitchen size and style may follow suit. Contemporary architects have generally favored the simple "pullman" kitchen which grew out of the necessity of space saving efficiencies mandated by the width of a railroad car minus the hallway. A couple of two-foot-deep counters separated by a three-foot walkway do the job. With two walking steps between the legs of the "work triangle" between sink, refrigerator, and stove, Pullman kitchens are efficient. They are also boring.

Remember, the kitchen is the hearth? It is the living space which most resembles the soul of the house, and it should "feel" that way. Every kitchen sink should absolutely have a window facing outside, or at the very least, a window to the immediate right or left when standing there. The more windows, the better, is a kitchen planners' mantra. There should be an adjacent table & chairs or at least a couple of bar stools at a counter for those not cooking to converse with. A fireplace or wood stove within view not only adds warmth and ambience but provides back-up to the cook-top and ovens. As an augmentation to under counter and overhead cabinets, a pantry (as in full height closet) is a blessing, and 3' x 3' (.9 X .9 meters) can hold a huge amount of everything.

Wait a minute! The kitchen is growing. No problem. A "U shape" or modified "L shape" requires additional floor space, but the benefits are evident if the kitchen is sensitively planned.

Enlarge the "U" shape a bit and there is sufficient space to locate a central "island" with a chopping block countertop and storage underneath. A larger size kitchen will be justified since everyone will congregate there.

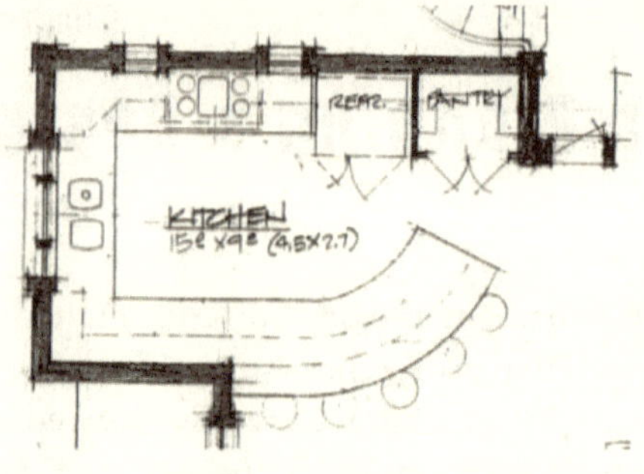

Kathryn's High Victorian has a relatively small kitchen. The curved countertop with leaded glass windows in the upper cabinet doors acts as a three-dimensional frame as viewed from the Great Room. Three small steps are all that is needed from the sink to refrigerator.

Kathryn's High Victorian Kitchen

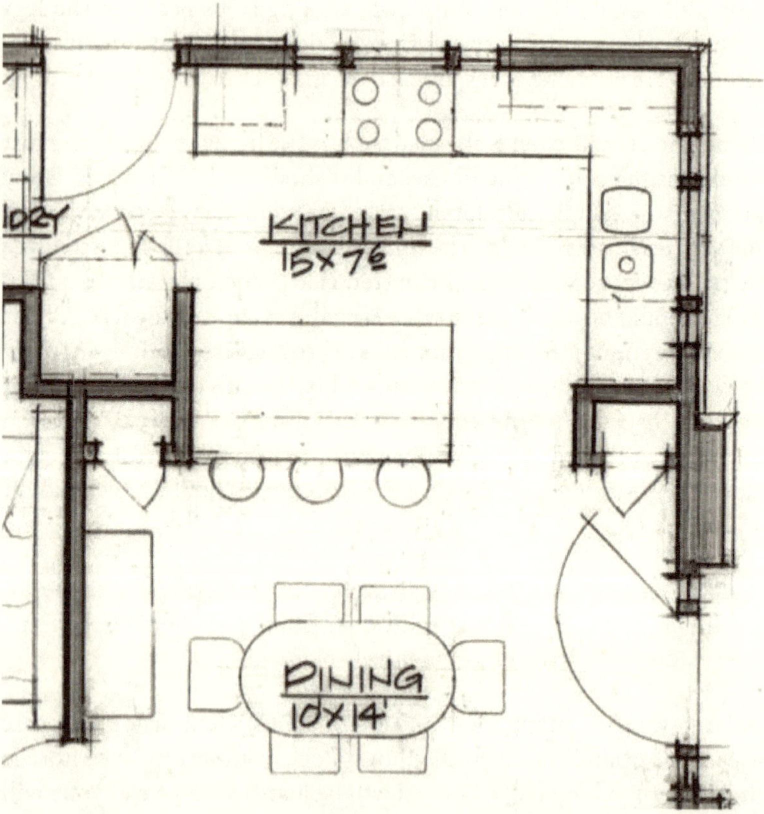

Bella Cabin has a small kitchen with two large windows and an open counter toward the Dining area. A full-size refrigerator (3' wide double door) is closeted to preserve visual scale within the room.

Chapter 16

Scale

Scale in Architecture is the perceived relationship by the observer, of the human body to architectural elements and spaces. This perception is more than just the relative sizes of things. Perception is also feeling, and feeling is difficult to quantify.

The famous Italian Renaissance Architect Antonio Palladio in the 1500's astounded the world by erecting huge fifty-foot square cubes and sticking ancient Greek temple fronts on all four sides. The central hall of these palaces was at least 20 feet high and everyone rich enough was immediately impressed and had to have one. When Thomas Jefferson designed his own Palladian mansion, Monticello, he prudently shrunk the entire house to a more livable size thus altering the "scale."

The typical suburban ranch style house in 1950's America, had rooms with 8' (2.4m) high ceilings, bathroom ceilings were 7' (2.1m) high, door heights were at 6'-8" (2m) Total livable floor area was about 1500 square feet (140 sq.m) for a typical three-bedroom house. During the following fifty years, sizes gradually expanded, not only in floor area, but also in volume. Even though the average size of adult occupants remained constant (except in girth), it was as if all houses were expanding like a child's beach ball on steroids. The living room had to be at least 12' (3.sm) high, the bedrooms 10' (3m), bathroom at 9' (2.7m), and the Lawyer foyer at least a respectable minimum of 16' (4.9m). Door heights increased to 8' (2.4m), possibly to ensure Shaquille's comfort should he happen to drop by. Bigger is better, right!

Wrong. Remember, scale relates to feeling and all these huge spaces may have served to impress the neighbors, but the sense of comfort and security was subsequently lost, especially for children. Curiously, when all interior spaces increase together, the sense of drama is gone. Contrast between stepping from under a low ceiling into a lofty room is more readily perceived sub-consciously even to the saturated and somewhat dulled sensitivity of modern man.

The future is bringing a renewal of human scale from a curious quarter, this being economics. As incomes dwindle, so will the sizes of one's home. Little houses are going to cost less, be demonstrably cheaper for air conditioning, but best of all; they will become cozy once again.

Paradise Manor

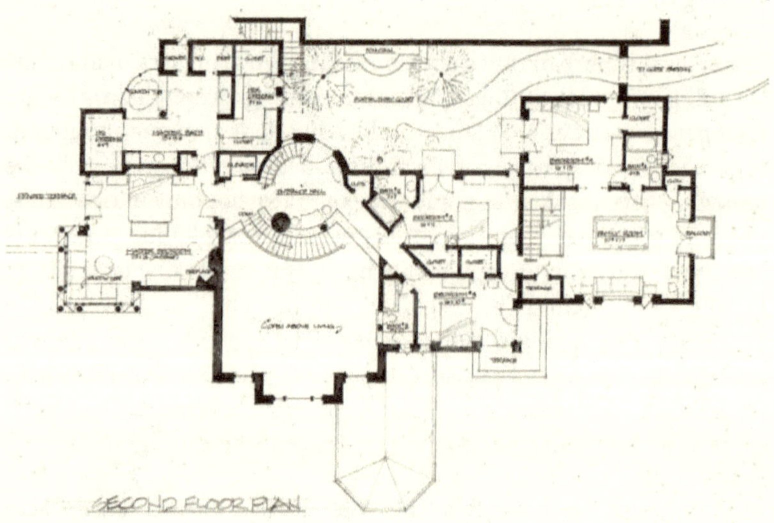

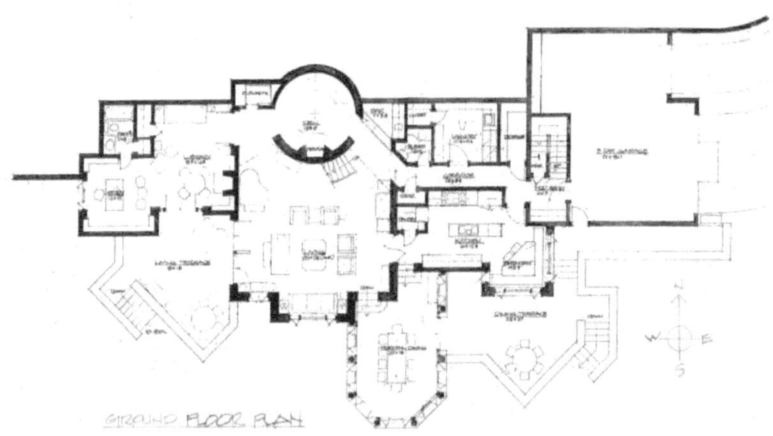

Some may consider it a bit of a push to rant about tiny houses, and then begin the chapter about scale with a house that contains a floor area of more than 5700 square feet (530 sq. meters) plus a three-car garage. The point is well taken, but there is an answer.

For a small house to be "homey" in the sense that living spaces all feel cozy and comfortable is almost a forgone conclusion. Except for glass "Boxitecture" dwellings, a single-family residence of less than a thousand square feet containing a family of four will by rote, be cozy.

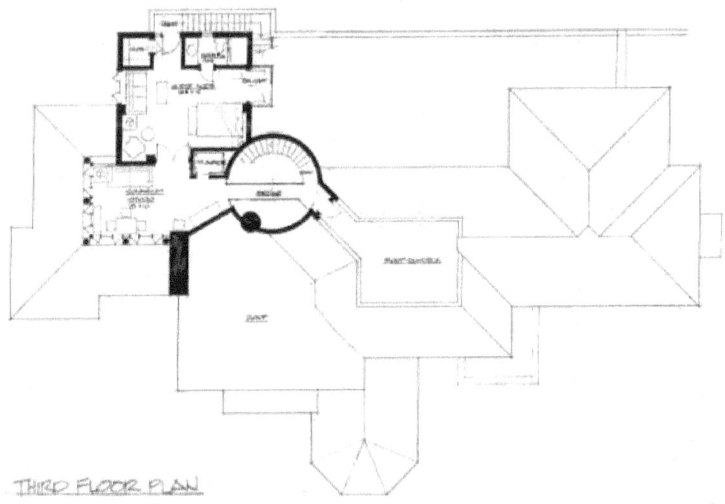

Although Paradise Manor has a large Entry/Living room, the remaining areas throughout the house are a progression of smaller spaces, each designed to express a unique and individual character.

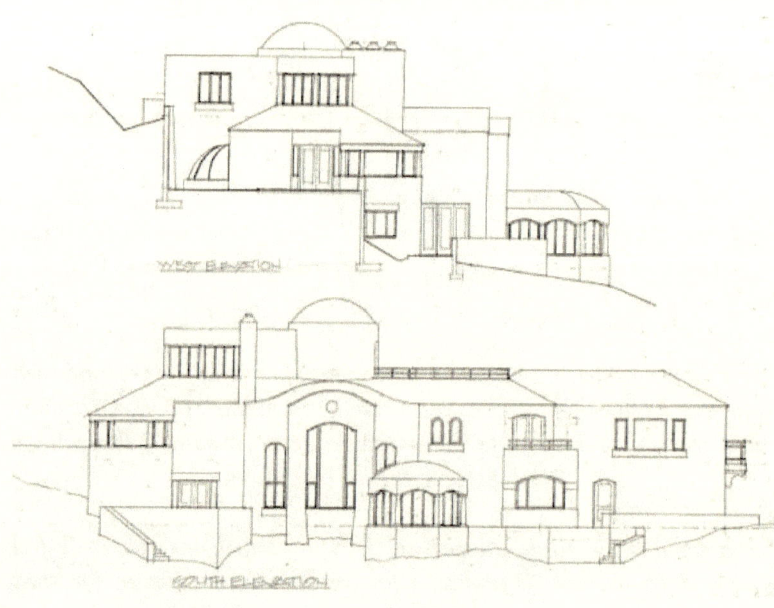

The East Elevation shows the Pedestrian entry gate to the Formal Entry Court. The North Elevation is actually a section cut through the Entry Court and through the outside stairway up to the third level Guest Suite and rooftop sun deck.

At the other end of the scale spectrum here is a tiny little cabin of less than 720 square feet (67 sq. m) that boasts 2 Bedrooms, 1 ½ Baths, and, comfortable living space.

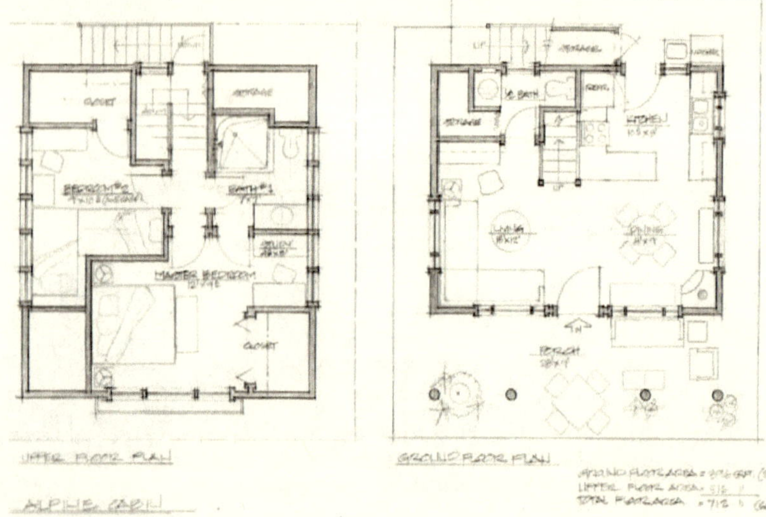

Chapter 17

Dining Room

People used to Dine. As a result, every house had a dining room. A hundred years ago it may have opened to the Parlor but was separated from the kitchen. With the disappearance of servants, and emerging of a less formal lifestyle, the dining room became used primarily for Thanksgiving and Christmas dinner. Open planned kitchens often now had a breakfast nook with table & chairs or a countertop with bar stools which were handy and thus preferred. In the 1950s the greatest, dual-purpose dining facilitator, the TV tray, was invented. Now the entire family could stuff their faces while stuffing their eyes full of Mork and Mindy. Recently, now that every bedroom has a computer, Junior and Sis need only grab something from the Fridge or microwave, then easily squat and gobble on their bed!

Living within a more home centered and basic lifestyle could very well be coming up in the cards for the middle class. Food procurement, preparation and consumption may become more of a focus of activity. So, the Dining Room may well re-assert itself as magnet for family togetherness so every small house should encourage that concept and contain a pleasing dining area.

Kay's Cottage

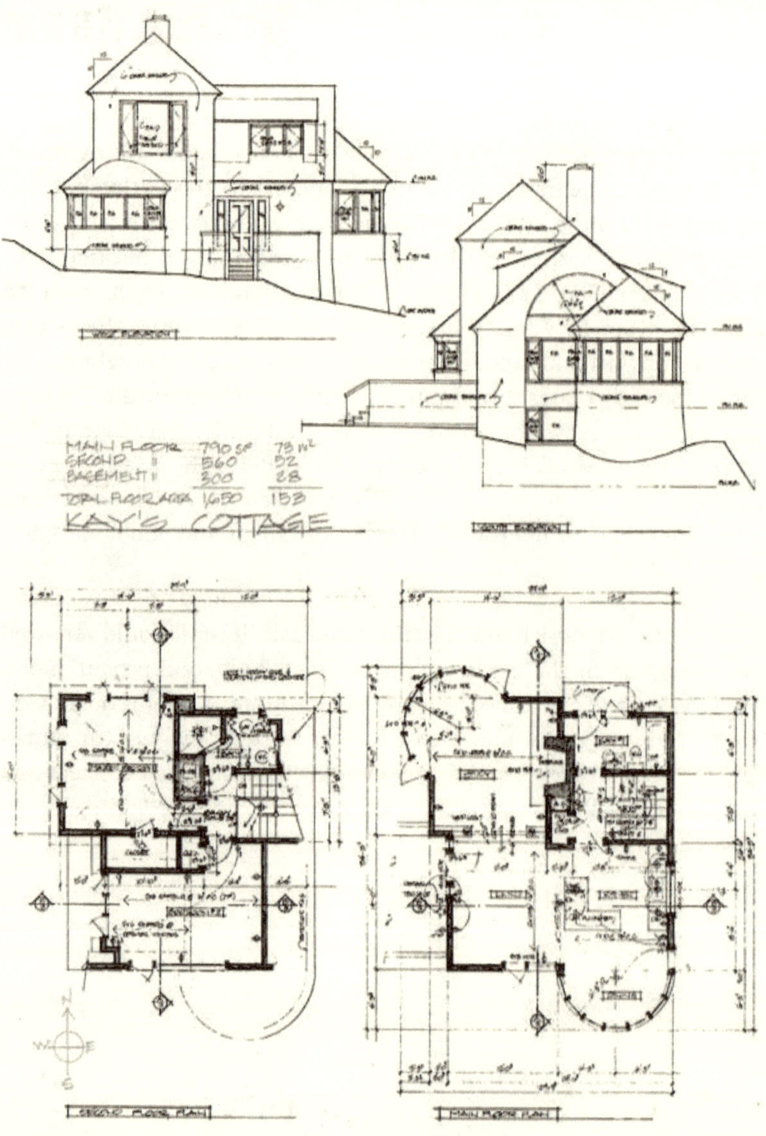

The Main floor flows from space to space with half round windows at each end.

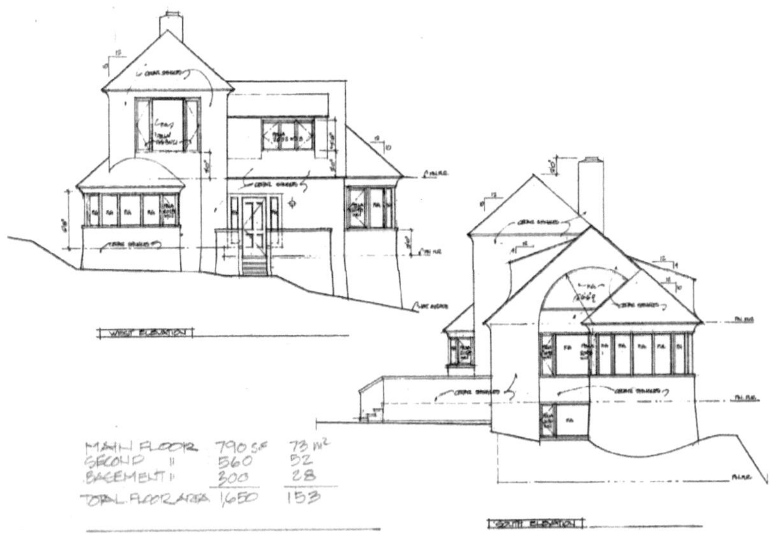

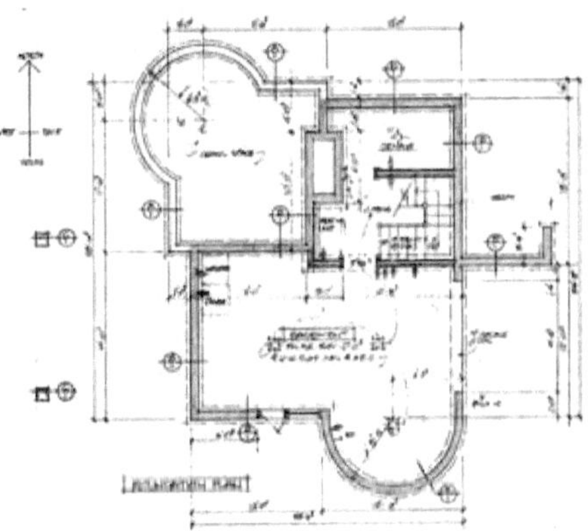

The basement level contains a single car garage and stair hall up to the Living areas. The under floor "crawl" space designated as unexcavated is used to distribute heating at the perimeter of exterior walls.

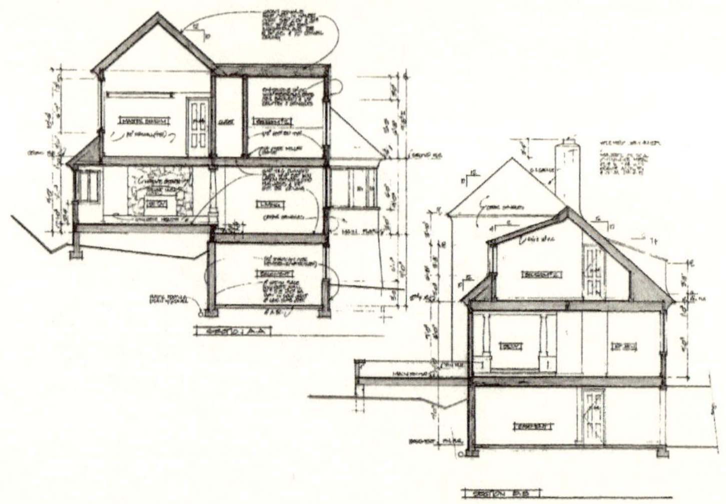

Section A-A shows the raised floor in the study which is used to create a cozier feeling near the fireplace. Various ceiling configurations and heights are also used to affect the mood within each space. The Living/Dining/ Kitchen area has an 8' (2.4 m) ceiling height which results in 7' (2.1 m) in the Study. The half-round window walls at both Dining and Study allow a panorama view toward the outside and emit balanced natural light to the interior.

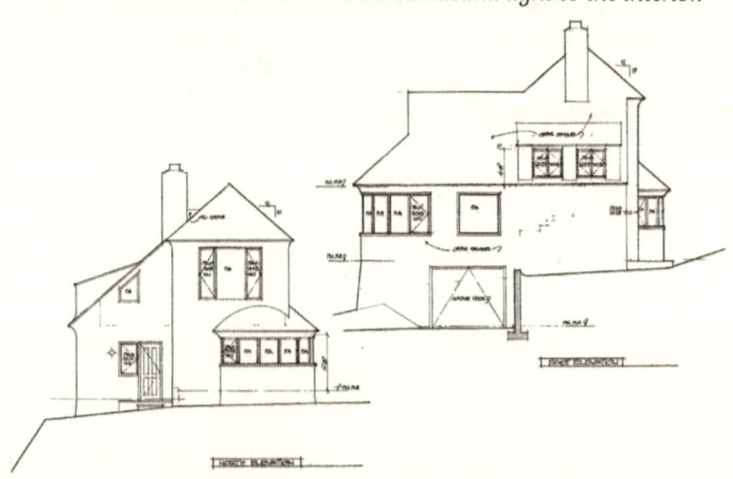

Kay's Cottage is designed within a version of what was referred to in the 1880s as Shingle Style. The entire exterior of the building including walls and roof is covered with wood shingles. This allows for a homogeneous character when expressing a complex massing of numerous elements of the structure.

Light

Light occurs in basically two varieties, Natural and Artificial. Natural is the best, but it only works during the day. At night we have always been forced to utilize the other one.

Actually, cavemen needed the other one during the day also, since punching out a side wall was not all too practical. Open windows required glazing in harsh climates and glass made from melted sand was known from ancient times. In medieval days, windows were tiny due to security concerns, plus glass was scarce and expensive. About the time that glass could have been more easily produced, thus cheaper, the government taxed it as a "luxury." This priced it out of reach of the common folk. Of course, you could go to church and see huge, lovely windows, but they were not suitable for home consumption by the masses.

With the invention of float glass and subsequent relaxation of the glass taxes, windows emerged onto the facades of buildings everywhere. They continued to be used in increasing amounts until today, many building exteriors are composed entirely of glass. Fortunately, the technology of combining multiple panes of glass, separated by inert gases, also enables large window areas to be relatively thermal efficient. This allows the potential for natural light in every well-designed room. Optimally, natural light needs to be abundant and diverse within habitable rooms, regardless of the use. The preferred way to accomplish this is using a multitude of windows located on walls and ceilings. Ideally, every room should have at least two windows that are located 90 degrees from each other. This helps to balance the light and mitigate glare. Obviously, the more windows on every wall and ceiling serve to approach that ideal. It is not necessary for the windows to go up to the ceiling, although, the higher, the easier it is to project light into the upper part of the room. Skylights and clerestories are highly recommended, especially if solid walls are mandatory.

Although contemporary Architects nearly always bring the windows down to the floor, the dog, cat, and cockroaches do not require a view. They all can crawl up on the furniture should they feel deprived. Raise the bottom sill up a couple of feet or more and not only will there be a wall to back up the couch too, but you may save the cost of tempering the glass. Position window size, location, and shape to frame a view and this will enable the window itself to be a visual focus as well as that which is outside. A full glass wall on a room may allow your Architect to get your house in a "Boxitecture" or "Shockitecture" magazine but it is a cop out. Every window, and door for that matter, should express something visually significant and often these features are the only elements available to give character to a simple design.

Vanessa's Lighthouse

Tinted and reflective glass of myriad types can augment character and aid air conditioning, but to save initial construction cost, clear crystal may be most sensible. An extensive overhang or shade device will keep the direct incidence rays of the sun off the glass and significantly hide the fact that you have not cleaned the windows for six months. Suffice it to say, natural lighting is the eye's best friend, and every room of every house should be comfortably bright, if possible, without artificial augmentation during daylight hours.

Then the sun goes down. The house now becomes a stage set and artificial lighting gives the designer an endless palate to create that which is seen. The building code requires minimum lighting levels for all uses within rooms. Irresponsible designers will just eggcrate fluorescent tubes in every office and sprinkle residential ceilings with recessed can fixtures (down lights). This is another cop out. The need for aggregate minimum task lighting is obvious, but that is just the beginning. Not only is the aspect of actual light rays but also the light fixture itself that lends ambience and mood to the space within. Every room, plus all exterior spaces provide surfaces for mounting light fixtures and the possibilities are as endless as one's imagination. Mount them on the ceiling, on the walls, under the cabinets, inside handrails, of every type and in every location. Use incandescent bulbs for a great mood setting (at least for a while), fluorescents to save energy, and LEDs to save even more energy while shredding your fixture budget. Your local lighting store is a candy shop for insulin deprived light junkies. The smallest house can become the grandest mansion through clever and creative lighting. Go for it.

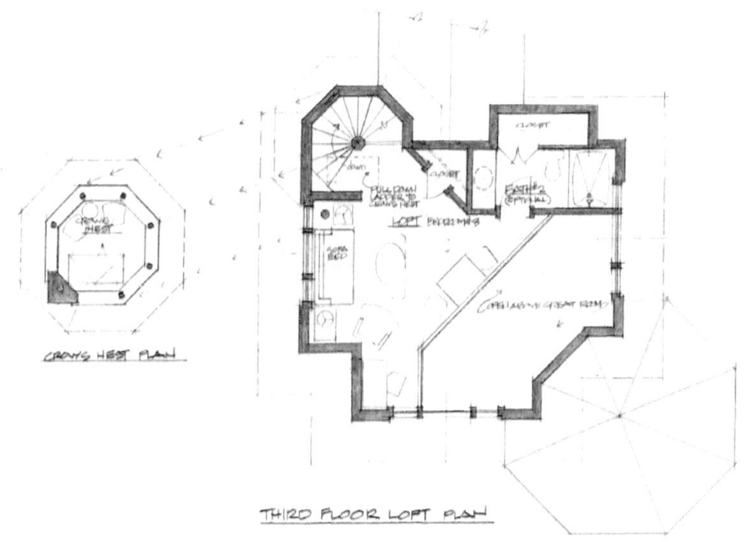

Vanessa's Lighthouse bathes in light. Windows are everywhere and stairs wind their way up to the Crow's Nest retreat and a 360 degree view.

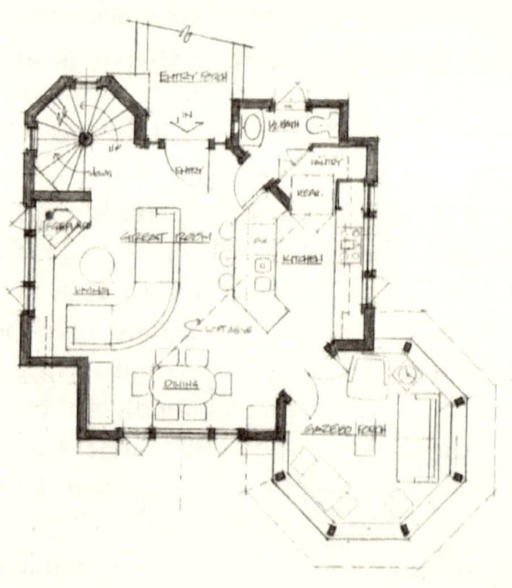

This, the main living level, is entered across a bridge. The 22 foot (6.7 m) square Great Room looks out to views in three directions and opens to an octagonal covered porch.

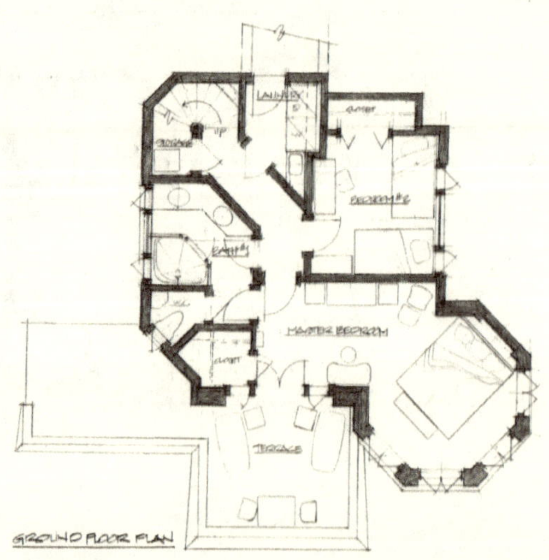

Interior livable floor space totals 1,580 square feet (147 sq. meters) plus covered porches comprise 280 sq. ft. (26 sq. m.). The plan contains 3 bedrooms including the third floor Loft, and 2 ½ bathrooms.

114

DOWNHILL ELEVATION

Chapter 19

Family Room

Within the less formal emerging living conditions after World War II, a little wooden collapsing gate was added between the Living Room and Foyer to keep the toddlers within view of the kitchen. One end of the kitchen expanded to become the Family Room and soon this area become the new living room by default. It was a sound idea since it resided toward the back of the house with big windows and glass doors to the adjacent covered patio, and fenced yard. Mom could command activities within and without. That was at least until she had to go get a job to support the whole thing. Then Guadalupe, the new housekeeper commanded but, what the heck, the family now had two cars, a boat, and two quads.

Downsizing the house in the future will see the emergence of kitchen/dining/family as a multi-use area contained within a single room. It still will be the heart of the house.

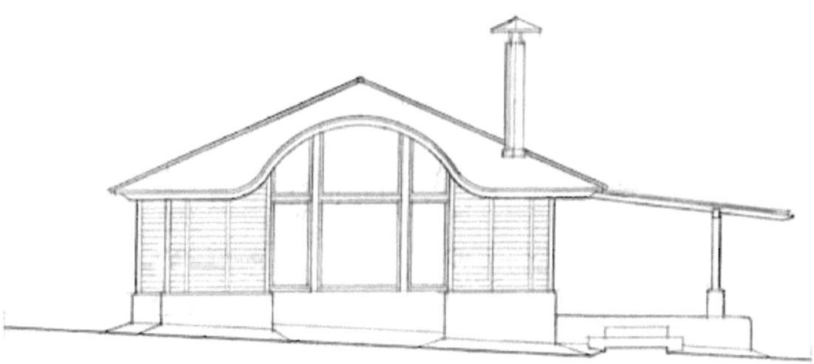

Here are a series of wood cabins beginning with this one-story, one-bedroom, one-bath house of a mere 807 square feet (75 sq. m). This is the basic floor plan of numerous little houses in this book; however, there are multitudes of differing Elevation styles available to tickle the fancy of Mom and for Dad to reach into his pocketbook.

The open "great room" concept results in a multiple use room over 35' (10.5 m) in length that ends in an important window to view garden or distant vista. The Dining area opens to a covered terrace plus there are optional decks off the Living area and Bedroom.

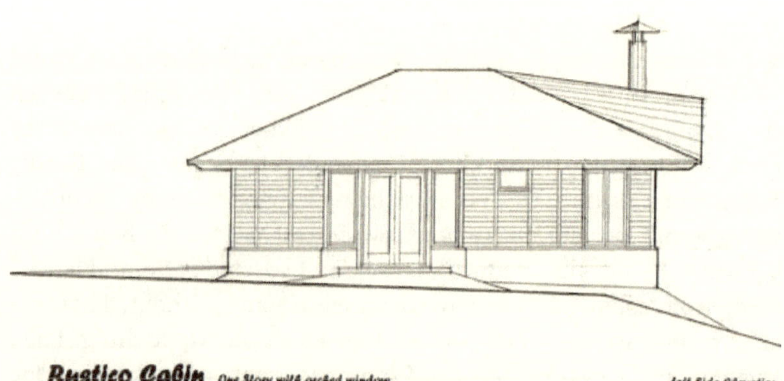

Rustico Cabin One Story with arched window   Left Side Elevation

The Left Side Elevation shows the double-glazed French doors and sidelight windows. The dramatic arched window at the front elevation gives a special dignity not usually found in such a humble residence.

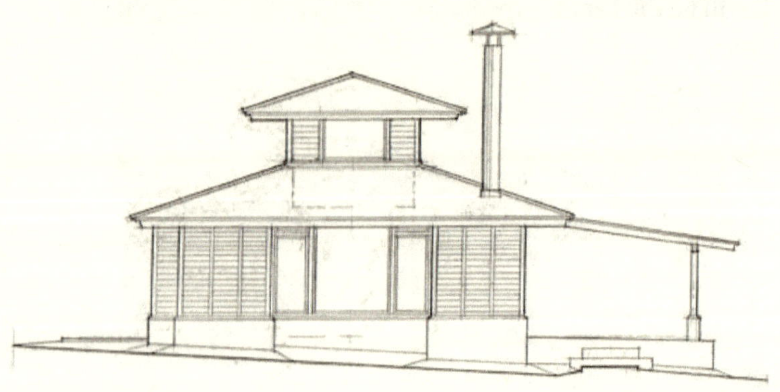

Rustico Cabin One Story with topknot   Front Elevation

To accommodate a second bedroom within the same floor plan, a Topknot is projected up through the center of the roof. This room enjoys a panorama view all around and is accessed by a spiral staircase from the Dining area. A topknot can be added to any attic area and is an inexpensive way to add an additional room. (See the Topknot on Bella Cabin, page 14).

The stucco covered wainscot rises up from the floor level to just under the windows. This allows for efficient moisture protection for a wood structure in wet climates.

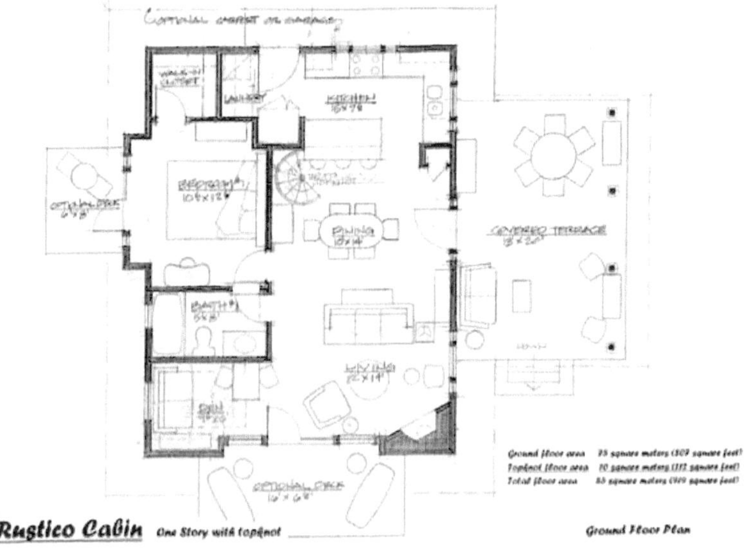

Rustico Cabin *One Story with topknot*

Ground Floor Plan

The access from the Dining area via the spiral staircase is shown above. A 4'-6" (1.4m) diameter circular set of stairs is a great boon to the inhabitants of little houses. Verify with your local City building department prior to their use, since code restrictions may apply.

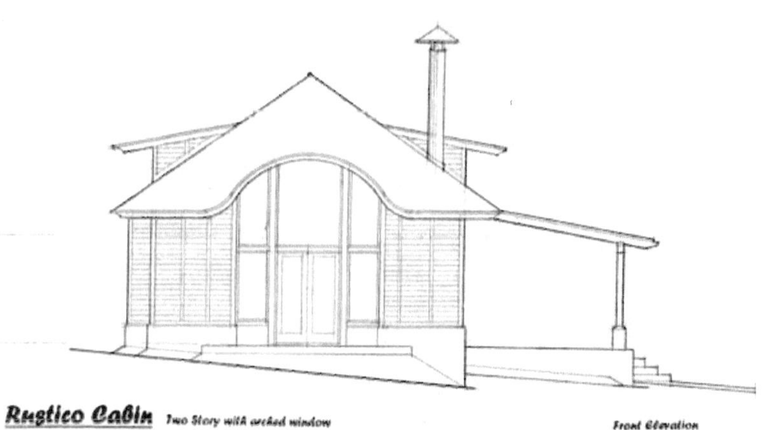

Rustico Cabin *Two Story with arched window*

Front Elevation

Just raise the exterior walls a bit and add a couple of eyebrows on the roof for Complete second story. By relocating the den upstairs, a full set of stairs marches up through the high ceiling Living area in order to access the Recreation Room and Bedrooms beyond.

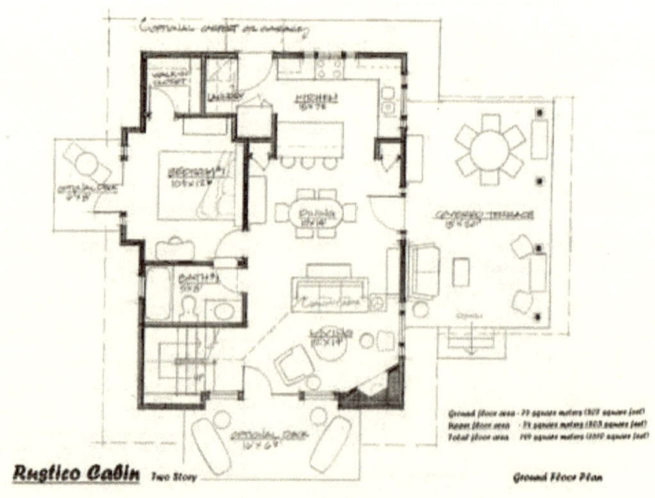

Rustico Cabin Two Story

Ground Floor Plan

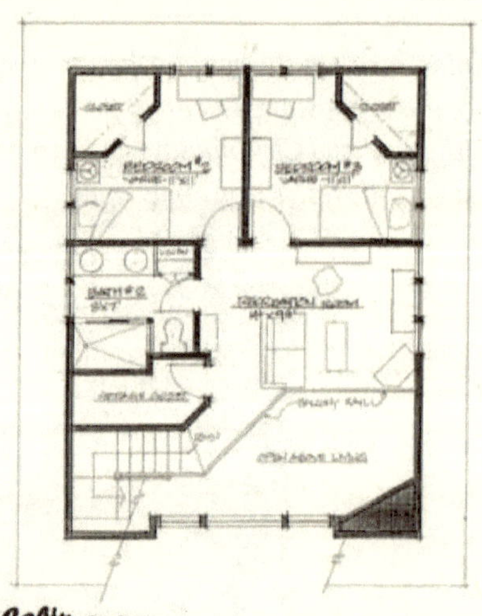

Rustico Cabin Two Story

Upper Floor Plan

The upper floor contains two bedrooms, a generous Bathroom, Recreation/ Den and ample storage. All rooms enjoy extensive windows for natural light and air.

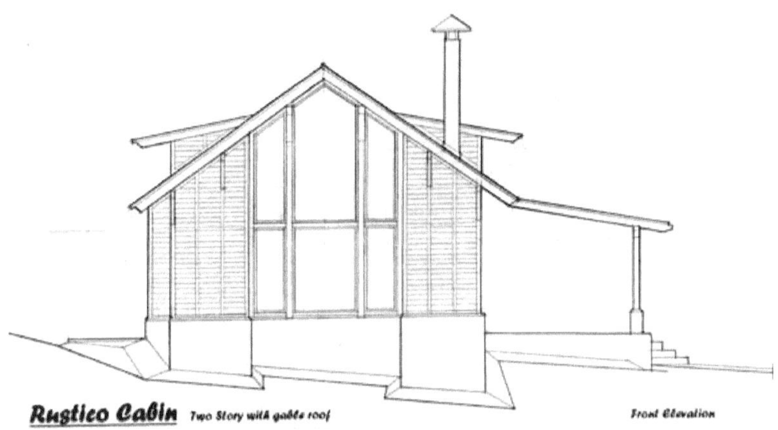

The two story version also offers a gable roofed elevation for a more traditional look.

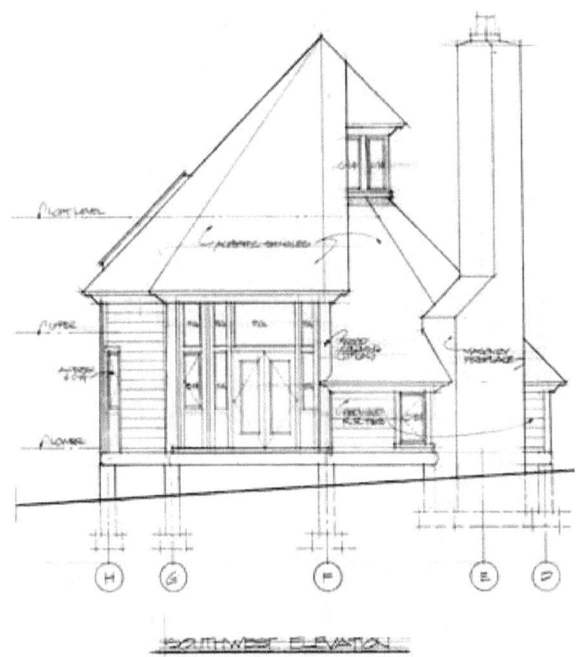

Cathy's Cabin

Not all houses need to be rectangular in floor plan. Octagons also work exceedingly well for small structures.

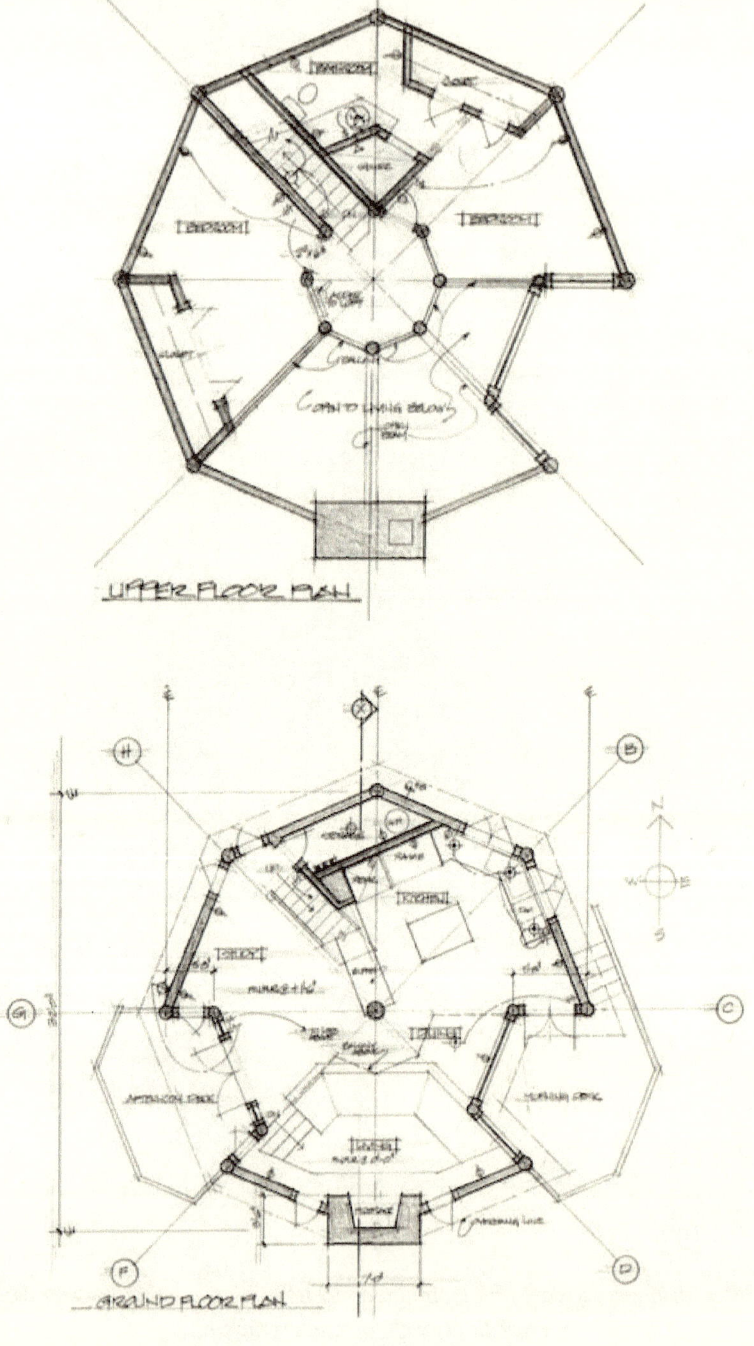
UPPER FLOOR PLAN
GROUND FLOOR PLAN

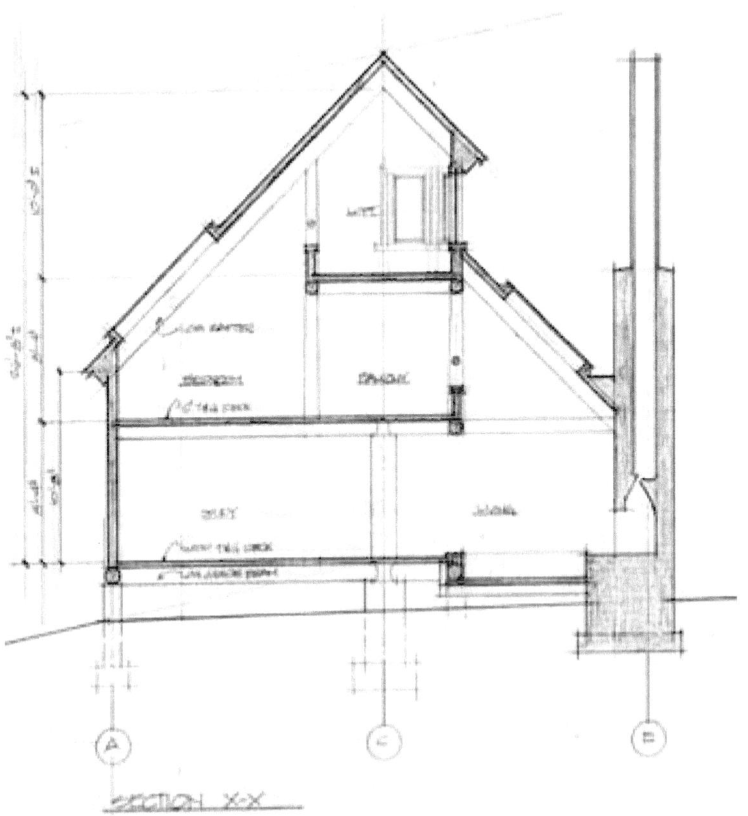

Cathy's Cabin has 1,100 sq. feet (102 sq. m) of floor area including a hideaway loft. A cost saving option would be to locate the fireplace (or a metal stove) adjacent to the loft balcony and substitute a metal stovepipe in place of the chimney.

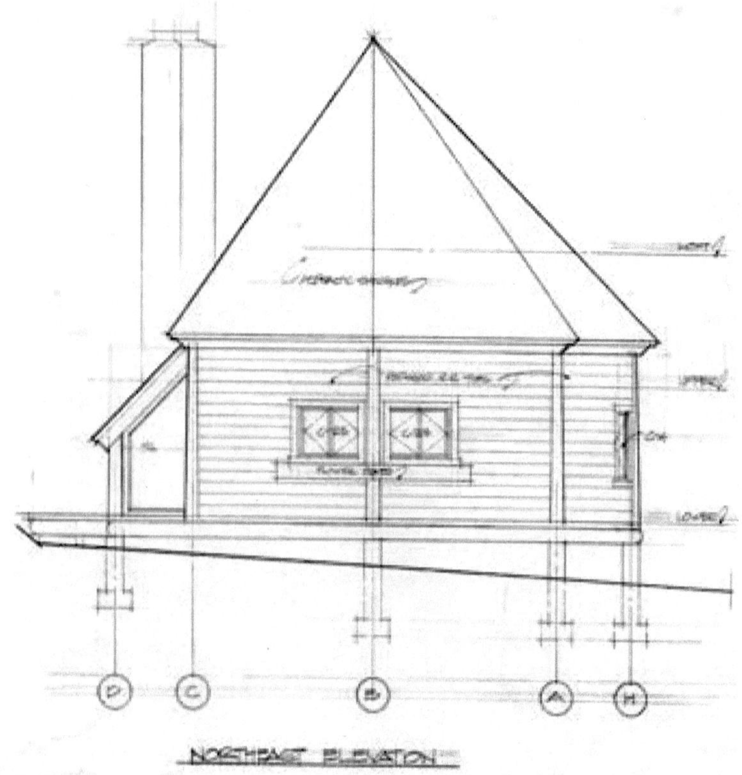

NORTHEAST ELEVATION

Chapter 20

Color

On an island in Greece is located the most wonderful hillside village that absolutely defines the word subtle regarding color. All houses in Mykonos are white. All other buildings are also white. All the walls leading up and down to the sea are white. Even most sidewalks and portions of all streets are white. Only there are splashes of bold blue color on windows and doors. One would think this color scheme to be too simple and thus boring. Because Mykonos is a compilation of little similar buildings scattered randomly against and on top of each other as they cascade down the mountain, the strong sunlight casts a riot of deep shadows everywhere. The shadows evoke the dynamic visual character that offers surprise and delight at the turn of every corner.

Within the homeowner's covenants of most housing developments today, exterior color selections are restricted to a limited palate to guarantee a visual unity to the neighborhood. This also prevents your next-door Philistine from covering his house to match the pumpkin from last Halloween. A Great Pumpkin next door could reduce the property values nearby, providing there is any left after the recent real estate bubble popped. Even the drapery linings on your windows (since they face outward to the street) are subject to restricted color selection and review by the homeowner's association board.

Fortunately, interior colors are left to the owner's discretion and your local hardware store can blend literally every color on the visible spectrum. As to what you choose, know that color enriches every mood, and so do not be afraid of considering any and all possible combinations. If your interior designer recommends that the entire inside is painted a simple "background" hue as a "blank slate for the furnishings and accessories," fire the piker. You need someone with more talent, especially if you are paying for them.

If you are unhappy with a color you have chosen, repainting is easy and inexpensive. Paint is the cheapest building material that also has the greatest ability to cover up a bad design or enhance a good one. If repainting the exterior still does not cover up the ugly façade, number two is landscaping in effectiveness. A trip to the local nursery will connect you to the real aspect of the "green" revolution.

Chapter 21

Bedroom

In early medieval times, the bedroom was a scant item, everybody talked, ate, lounged, played, sang, danced, slept, choked the bishop, and insured their respective progeny on top of a disgusting heap of straw inside the castle's Great Hall. Eventually, the lady of the house, perhaps tiring of Cousin Jerald's repeated attempts to ascertain just how far her legs went up there, or maybe the lord, just in need of a wee bit of privacy added a second floor within the hall and the bedroom was, er' conceived. By the early 20th century, the average middle class suburban house contained at least a couple of bedrooms, generally on a second-floor level. Parents occupied the greater of them while numerous children shared the remainder, usually separated by gender. Each bedroom contained a bed or two, a washstand with bowl, a wardrobe, dresser and a chamber pot under the bed. Sometimes there was a single bathroom to be shared by all but often there was an "outhouse."

Coincidental with suburban housing after World War II, the size of bedrooms became a bit larger and had a built-in, walk-in or wardrobe closet. Parents enjoyed a private bath, and the other bedrooms shared a second. The 1960's brought the Hippie's mandatory waterbed which at 7' x 7 California King Size required an increase in room dimension and re-evaluation of the structural attributes of the second floor. Things remained similar until the emerging housing Boom-Bubble of the 1990s. Then everyone went nuts and the egocentric driver mania became the focus of the Master Bedrooms evolution to a "suite." Even though most parents only still slept there, the Suite mandated a dressing room, an exercise alcove, his and her bathroom, a whirlpool and often an adjacent study for a couple of computers. "Size matters" since the ever-increasing real estate "flipper" syndrome mandated it to guarantee increasing property values. Certainly, it followed that every child has a personal "mini-suite" containing bedroom, study, and bath plus the same for any guest or two.

Now that reality has adjusted per future housing aspirations, common sense will guide where we sleep and the follow up will be fewer and less grand bedrooms. Lofts within the cathedral ceiling will point back to those days of yesteryear and the Murphy bed, pull out sofa and trundle will perhaps reawaken us to a cozier tomorrow.

Casa Jeanne

A Master Bedroom Suite need not be large to be spacious. Casa Jeanne has a bedroom of only 11' X 13' (3.3 X 4 m) yet with a high-pitched roof facing a private covered balcony framed by windows, it is cozy and dignified.

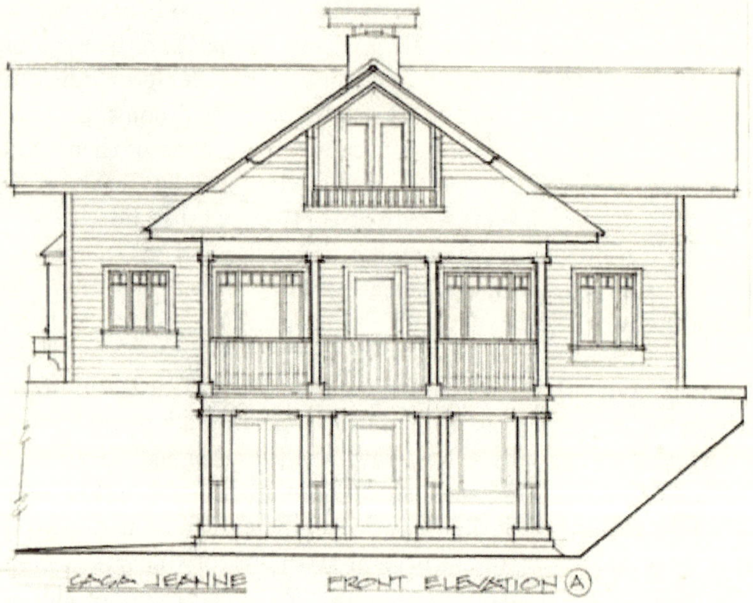

The style above echoes a Midwestern American farmhouse, only on a mountainside.

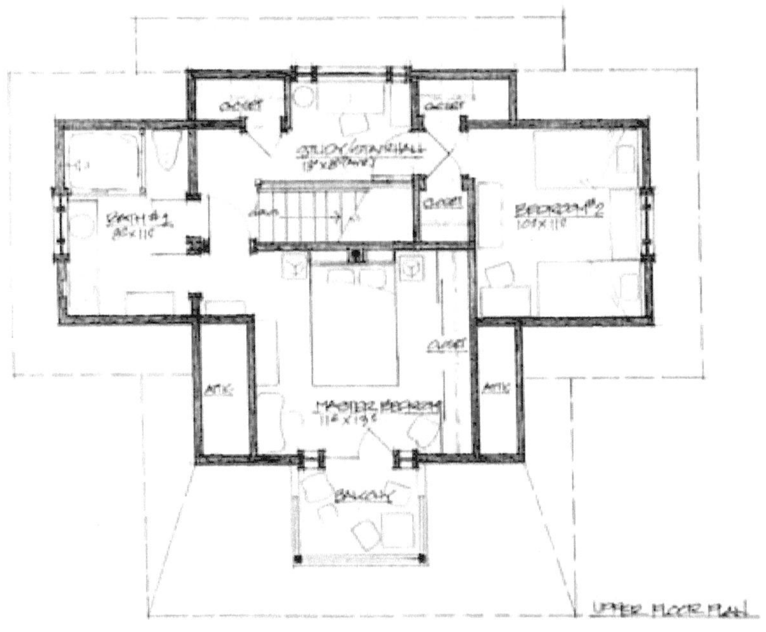

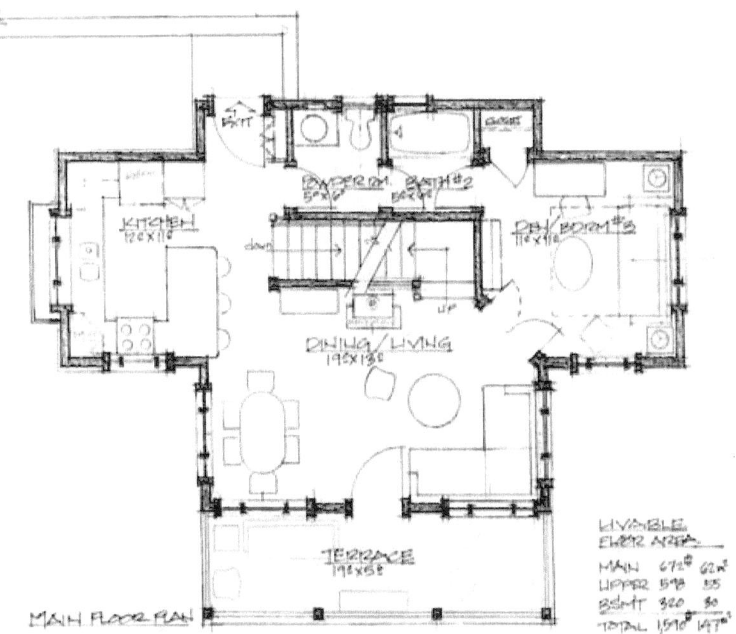

The entire Main Floor is a single flowing space using the staircase as a visual focus.

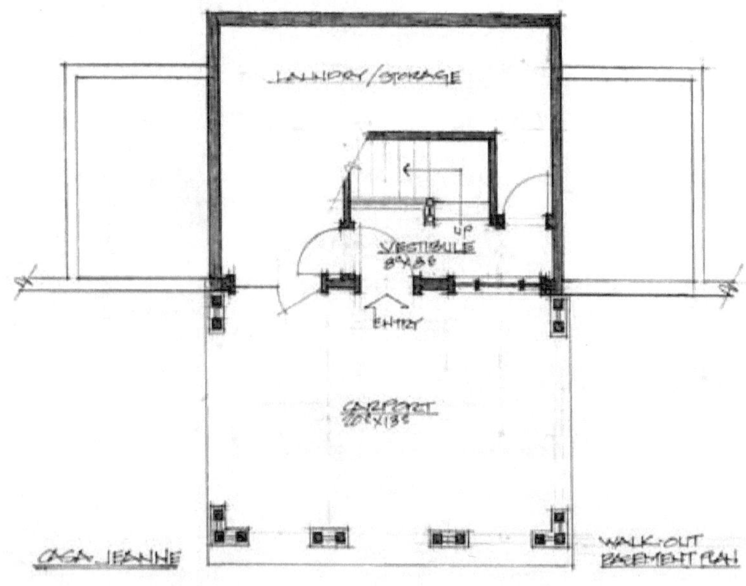

The walk-out Basement opens onto a large carport which doubles as a party terrace.

Here are a Neo Craftsman style with stucco finished base and logs above.

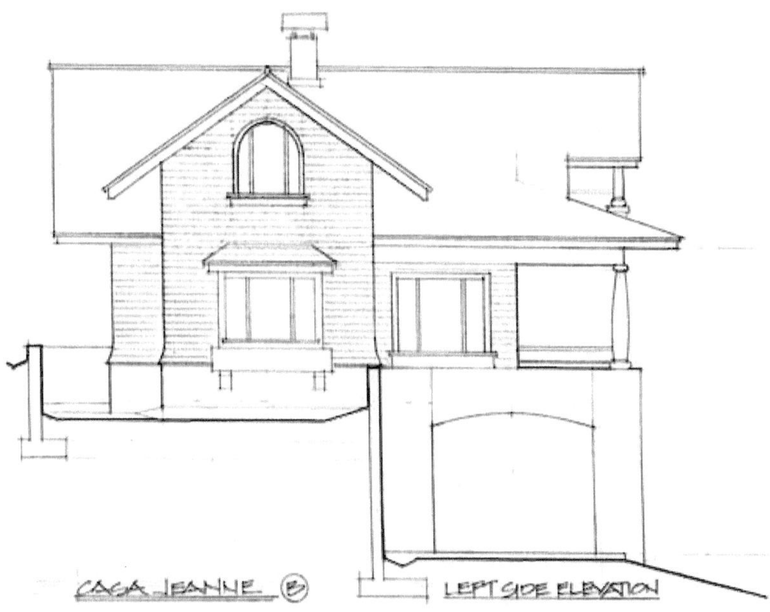

CASA JEANNE B
LEFT SIDE ELEVATION

Chapter 22

Energy

Energy is always in the news. Embracing the future, lack of energy, or at least the increasing cost of same, will likely define the size and method of constructing houses. Residential heating and cooling are the most consumptive uses of energy and in more harsh climates, careful and thoughtful efforts are needed to gain maximum effectiveness regardless of the energy source. Since today's electronics and lighting systems consume relatively minor amounts of power, a small solar array is sufficient for an entire house. Heating and cooling is another matter, and here the volume of interior spaces and insulation value of the enveloping structure are paramount. If you build a house with a smaller footprint and utilize lower ceilings, the building will not only cost much less to create physical comfort, but emotional comfort will follow.

Next, insulation is critical. Double and triple pane windows are an excellent investment. Regardless of the structural system of the building, ceilings, walls, and yes, floors should be heavily insulated and effectively weather sealed. This first line of thermal defense is the common-sense default concept for any building.

Once the building is efficiently designed, the choice of energy to provide air conditioning relates to that which is readily available locally and at a reasonable current price, whether that be electricity, gas, or fuel oil. In more rural areas, backup wood heating and even wood fired cooking is a sensible alternative. A well-designed fireplace (see Count Rumford) also adds a great sense of well-being, especially when combined with a cup of hot spiced wine.

There are countless books that offer information about passive solar design, straw bales, rammed earth, pop bottle walls, adobe, Cobb construction, and even ancient wattle and daub. Expanded polystyrene foam is a brilliant material wherein a complete structure, including roof, walls, floors, and even the foundation may be quickly erected and finished utilizing only a plastering contractor. The foam method is fire resistant, earthquake resistant, mold resistant, water resistant, amazingly strong, and no critters will want to eat it. The primary attribute of the foam, of course, is its tremendous insulation value. The only drawback is the difficulty of the public to actually believe that a Dixie Cup house can be strong enough to withstand the elements. Certainly, however, when you are freezing your fanny off in your concrete block house and the neighbor next door is toasty in his little Foam Fantastic dwelling, you just might consider a bit of add-on retrofit foam to your outside wall surface and ceiling.

There is an entire spectrum of permutations and combinations to blend within an energy efficient house concept and no single system is best for all. Realtors are always saying, "Location, location, location," which to the point, might be food for thought. If one prefers to completely solve the air conditioning, simply move to a location within about ten degrees of the Equator and then just walk up any mountain until you find your preferred year-round temperature, and there you are.

Desert Deco

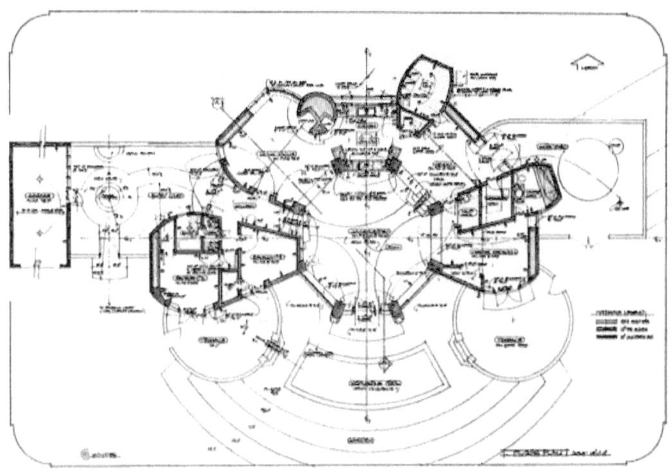

This is a passive solar design for hot arid climates. The building is partially buried within the ground with descending terraces leading past a pool to the Conservatory. Thermal mass of the earth acts as a natural "flywheel" to automatically modulate extreme climates. The octagonal Conservatory is covered by a semi-translucent fabric roof.

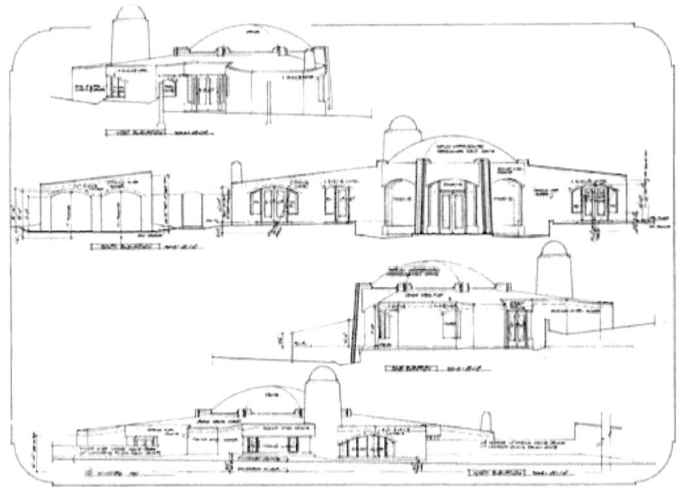

This is a huge solar collector and when covered with another fabric shade cloth. serves to shade and humidify the garden below. Air is distributed under the floors of adjoining rooms, through double exterior walls, and back through the attic with direction and venting of the air to be varying depending upon whether cooling or heating is required.

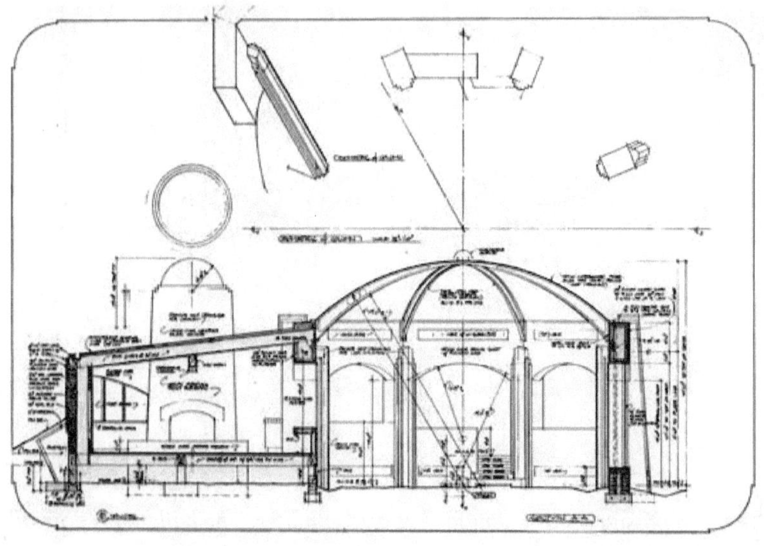

Chapter 23

Bathroom

That which goes on in the bathroom tends to be private and some quite disgusting stuff results. That is why prior to the flush toilet, that particular bodily function was relegated to a four-by-four shack located generally, 20 seconds away on dead winters run and preferably downwind.

When the outhouse was finally brought indoors, thanks to a pressurized piped water supply, the disgusting element was largely removed by a simple device called a "P" trap. Whoever first named this device most likely was semi-literate since this automatic water valve more accurately resembles a fallen down "S." None the less it continues to prevent noxious gasses from rising from the sewer up into the room and lies under sink, lavatories and within the body of flush toilets.

The suburban house of the 1950s usually sported two bathrooms, the grander reserved for the Master Bedroom and the second allotted to be shared by the remaining bedrooms. The shared bathroom typically was 5' x 8' (1.5 X 2.4m) and contained a lavatory/basin with storage under the cabinet, a toilet and combination bathtub/shower. These baths were built by the millions and both little Junior and Sis probably experienced playing with their rubber duck in the bathtub and later junior playing with something else while sitting on the toilet. Not to be denied, sis more than likely awakened a first tingle from a drip of the bathtub faucet.

Master Bathrooms typically were always larger, containing two lavatory basins with a huge mirror over, a separate alcove for the toilet and often both a stall shower and separate bathtub. As the progress of fashion dictated, the Master "suite" bathroom expanded in size and height. By 2000 ceilings were consistently 9 feet high (2.7m), the bathtub become a huge sunken pool, surrounded with marble and a motor to blow bubbly water under the surface. The shower stall became a glassed-in room with a stainless-steel column centered on one marble covered wall which sprayed a chorus of variable water jets from head to toe. Fashion dictated that the lavatory top with basins be raised another 6", maybe to a accommodate dad who happened to play NBA basketball. Normal peoples' elbows dripped water on the floor now, but everybody was doing it. The sensible location of sinking the basins into the lavatory top became "uncool." Now everyone must put the basin on top of the counter, and often the "mixing bowl" must be of clear glass so everyone could see the green ring of slime gathered under the counter where the bowl met the surface. What price Vanity?

Bathrooms in little houses of the future will be fewer and of smaller size. The old standby 5' x 8' will emerge again. The "Jack & Jill", which separates the tub/shower from the lavatory/toilet by a door thereby allowing access from two directions, will increase in favor. Thoughtful architects and designers will increasingly study innovations from the boat and travel trailer industries where the tune "less-is-more" philosophy actually has relevance. Marine Architects have always used their "heads" when designing heads. Surf of the Airstream website will astonish you with numerous methods of utilizing a shower stall as a complete bathroom at once functional and beautiful to boot.

The bathroom is arguably the room with the fewest moments of occupancy, so a couple more minutes while waiting for Sis to get out of the shower will, of necessity, be endured.

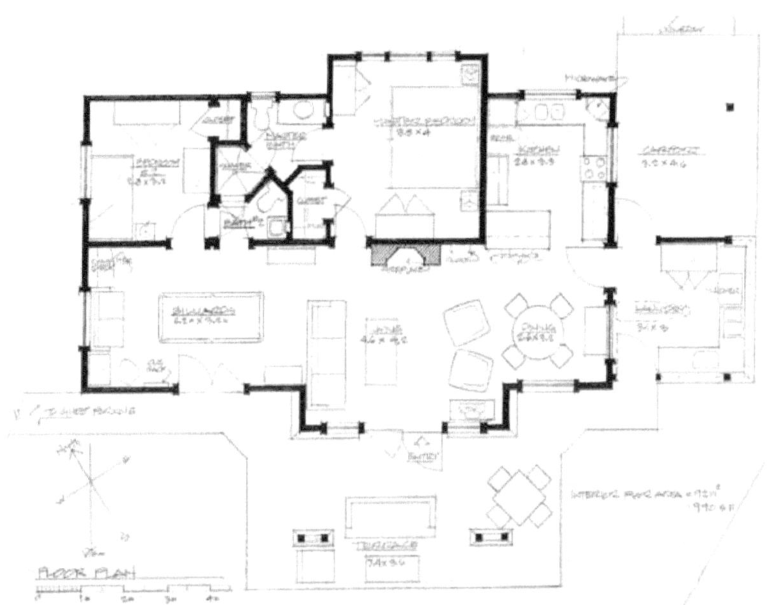

Casa Adriana

A close look at this Floor Plan shows a radical, yet simple departure in efficient Bathroom design. Everyone wants a private Master Bath solely for the use of the Master Bedroom. Other Bedrooms also prefer to enter directly into a bathroom. In most polite societies, it is absolutely preferred for guests to enter a bathroom without walking through a bedroom. Here, all these requirements are met within a small 10' X 10' (3 X 3m) square. There are even two closets included in the mix. The key is a shared shower with two frosted glass doors.

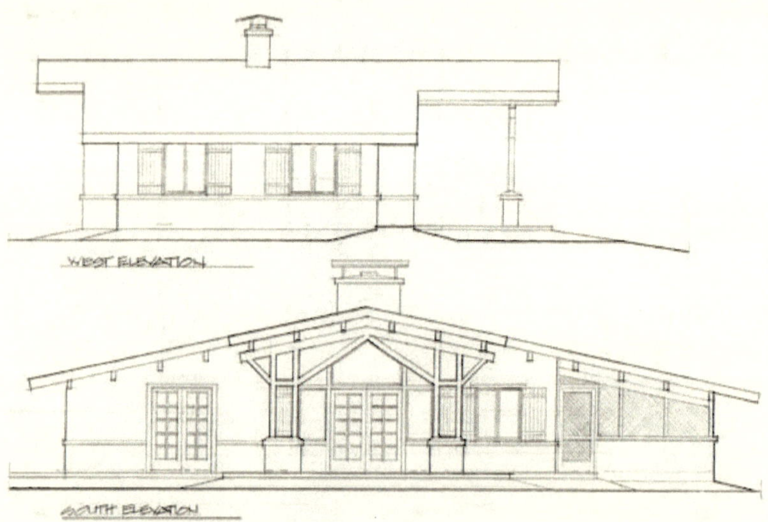

Casa Adriana is a two-bedroom house of less than a thousand square feet (90 sq. meters) livable and still can accommodate a pool table.

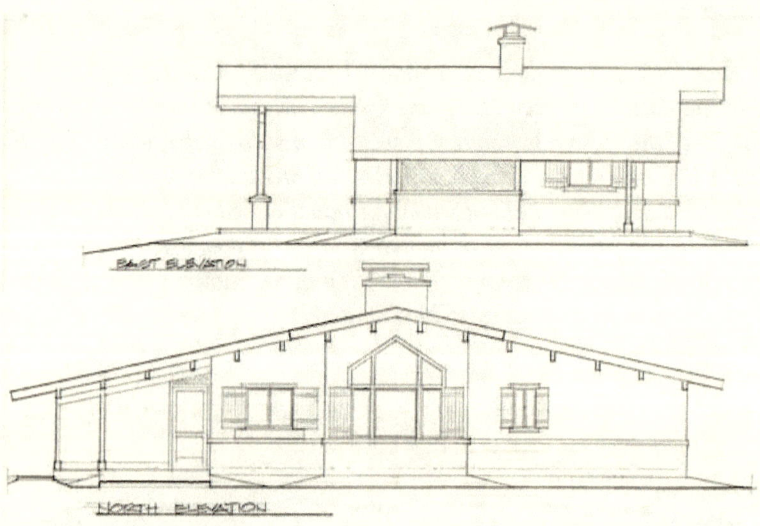

The house is extra wide and skinny to embrace a view and allow for a large covered front porch.

Chapter 24

Water

Water is life. No discussion about sustainable living patterns can commence before first establishing a suitable source of potable water for every site. Within the "civilized" world today water is available hot or cold, at the touch of the tap and taken completely for granted. Great pains are taken by governing bodies to ensure an adequate supply for those they are responsible for, and with burgeoning populations, the future will bring this increasingly difficult.

Once an assured water supply is established for a new house, it is the responsibility of the owner to absolutely guarantee that every drop is efficiently utilized and if any is discarded, that the waste is properly treated. This is not difficult providing the house and lot is designed within a holistic system, and the local building codes do not prevent sensible water management. If your house is connected to a municipal water system, you will not have any say regarding the quality of the incoming supply. This water will be chlorinated, probably fluoridated, and other items will be added according to local governmental protocols. This water may taste a bit weird but it likely will be safe. Should your property be in a remote location, you just may be blessed with good ground water and if rights to use it have not been sold off to some predatory investor, you are in luck. Before you use this ground water, turn on the faucet but don't hold a match to the spigot, just in case that derrick on the adjacent farm is stirring things up down below. You may also live in an area where there is sufficient continuous rainfall and allow your roof to act as your well. A simple gutter, downspout and attached cistern is infinitely less expensive than even a shallow well but be certain that the local government allows you to use the rainwater. Some don't. In many arid areas in the USA, it is code required for a certain percentage of rainfall to be retained on-site within graded bermed "catchments". This is an excellent idea to plant these catchments with edible plants.

Once you have used the water, what do you do with it? Residential wastewater is of two principal varieties, Grey and Black and constitutes what is referred to in the technical lingo as "effluent." Black effluent is that which goes from the toilet and must be treated prior to distributing it into the environment. The city does it for you and charges you a bit for the service. If you have the proper treatment plant on your property, you can biologically make it pure and re-use it for drinking or at least for the garden, that is, if they will let you. Many cities will not let you, since they have contracted the effluent to a third party for some sweetheart deal of their own. Then there is grey effluent. This is all wastewater other than Black effluent. This is bathwater, washing machine outflow, and all the remainder that goes down the drain. Throughout most of the world, this grey effluent is diverted directly onto the garden where it turns the lawn green and most sensibly, nourishes the veggies. Not in the USA. Once again, the city fathers cite some obscure health regulation and require that the Grey be blended with the Black and passed on (as it were) for treatment. The unbelievable lunacy of a taboo against utilization of human waste, properly treated, and added to food growing belies incredulity.

Tried and true effluent treatment technology has been utilized the world over for centuries and a brief session on your favorite search engine will acquaint you with numerous inexpensive little house sized systems for total recycling of your wastewater. A bit of research is certainly time well spent.

Casa Emily

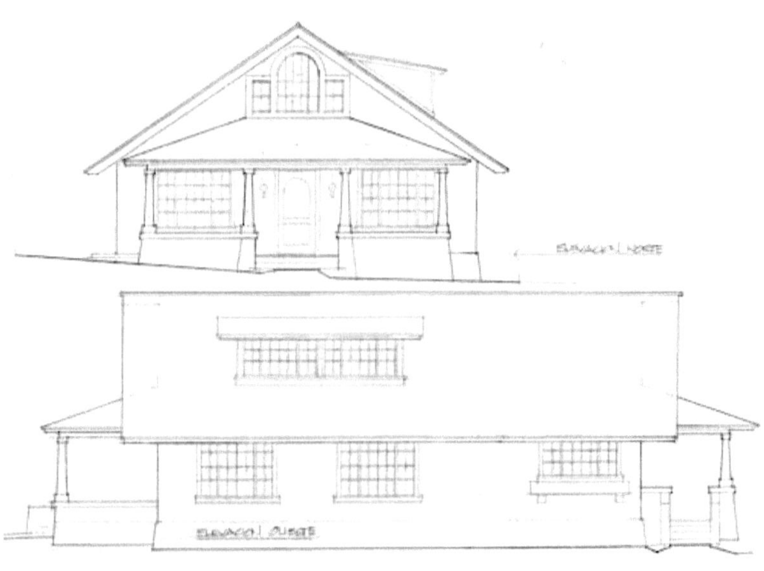

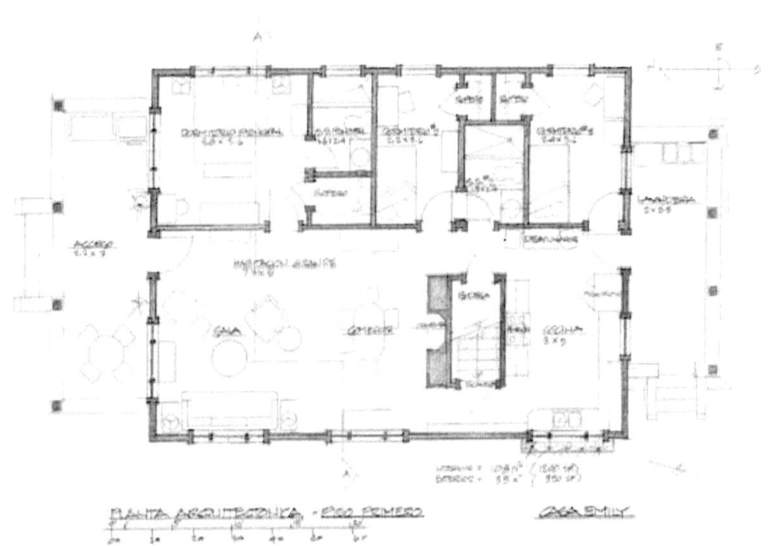

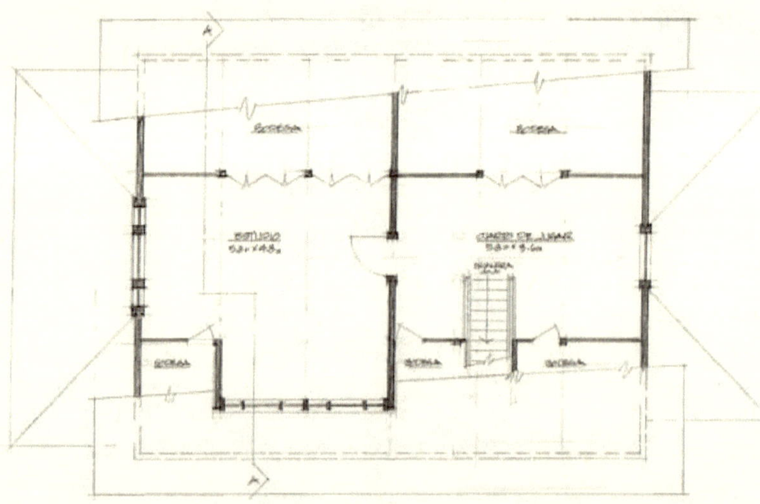

Casa Emily has a big surprise with two spacious rooms plus storage in the attic. The Estudio (Studio) enjoys two spacious windows. The 3-Bedroom, 2-Bathroom house totals a living area of 1200 square feet (108 sq. meters) plus two covered porches.

This house is similar to many in Costa Rica of 60+ years ago with the exception that there would have been a hallway running through the center from front to back porches.

The Open Plan concept fortunately has arrived, thus allowing for increased openness within a small and tidy floor plan.

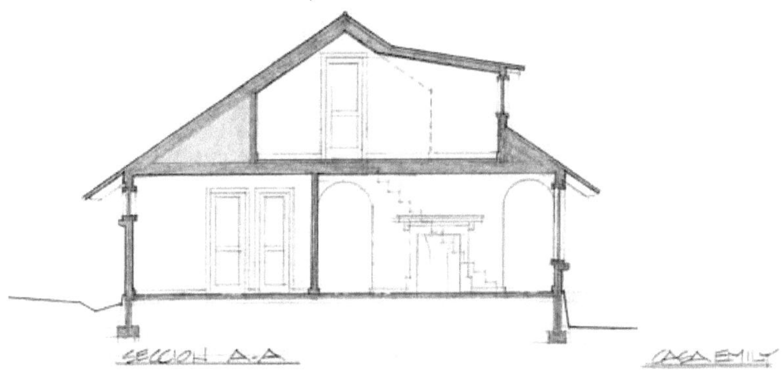

The section above demonstrates how additional living space can be created by putting a floor on the attic and adding windows to each gable end of the building. A raised eyebrow dormer window along the roof side allows for a second row of natural lighting. As can be seen, generous amounts of storage space remains where the attic ceiling line is lower than four and a half feet (1.4 meters).

Anne's Cabin

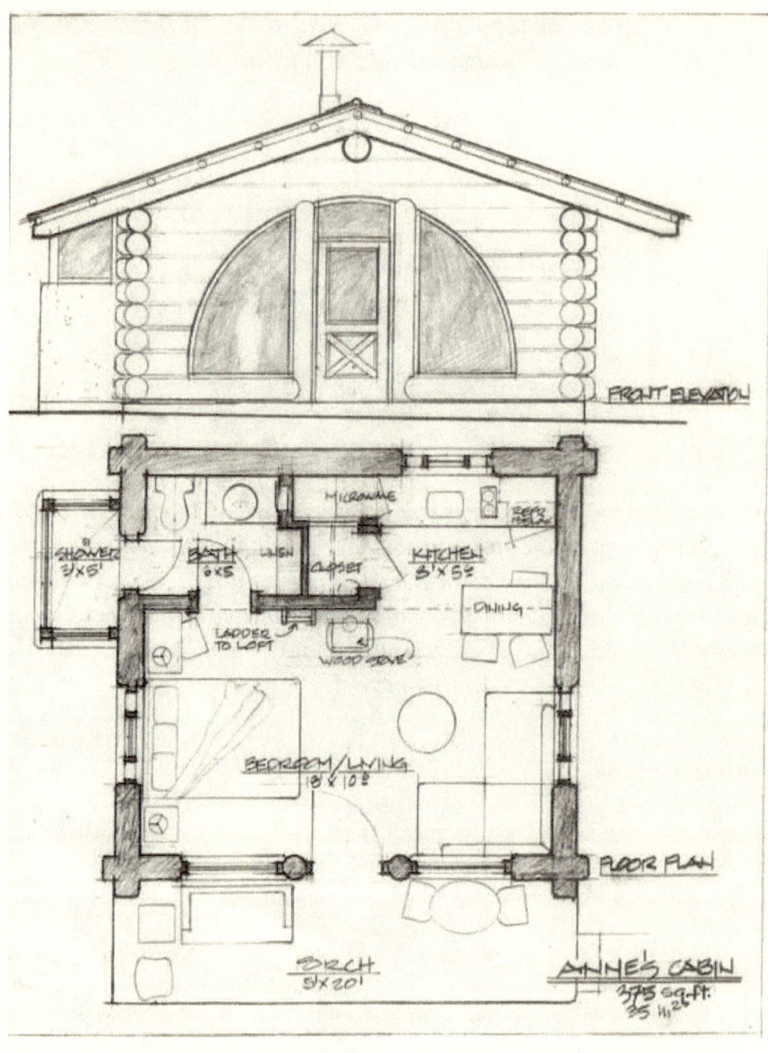

Anne's Cabin is the next-to-smallest house in the book but what it may lack in size, it makes up for in Grand Presence. The external dimensions are a mere 20 X 18 feet (6 X 5.5 meters). There is a sleeping loft above the Bath and Kitchen containing a double bed which allows a party of five adults to slumber in rustic comfort.

146

Chapter 25

Laundry

A few steps behind the back porch used to be a little small building called the "wash house" where grandpa would stoke up a fire under a big kettle and grandma would boil the clothes in lye water. She then would hang them all up, sometimes including grandpa, outside in the sun to dry.

Things have come a long way until now, all that is needed for a huge home is a 6' x 6' little room containing an automatic washer and automatic dryer. Yes, automatic is the key word and both these appliances are wonderful. They are so simple, even the kids can do it. That is if mom can coerce them. Thanks to the wondrous evolution of modern fabrics, that other former mainstay in the laundry room, the iron with ironing board has all but disappeared. Now Mom can get another "outside" job to help for Junior and Sis's college education. Since your automatic clothes dryer requires considerable energy, whether electric or gas, there is a tried-and-true method from the past. This item is called the "clothesline" and only requires a bit of dry air and sunshine to power it. The clothesline also just happens to be a bit more holistic, since air drying and sunshine aid in disinfection plus render your clothing a sweet scent. Be careful that your neighbors do not see you doing this however, since you probably will be in violation of your homeowner's covenants. Using the automatic dryer may be less expensive than a lawsuit, since sneaking out at night to hang up the laundry negates the benefit of the solar aspect. While you are at it, you better muzzle your chickens; they will also be in violation.

Bonita Cabin

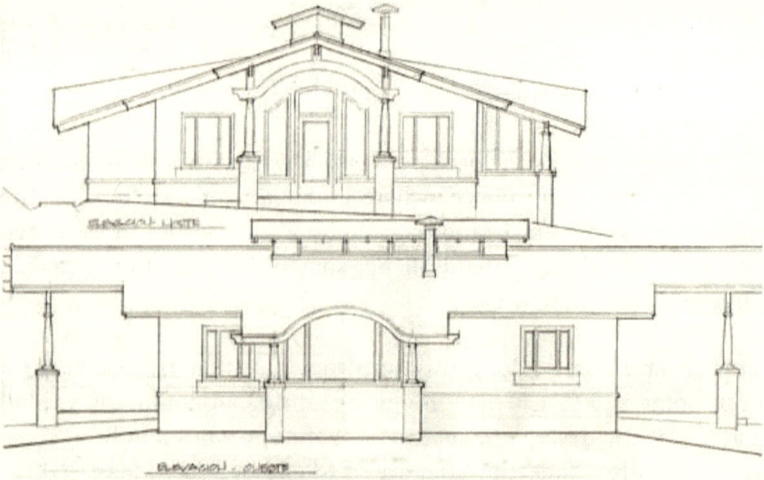

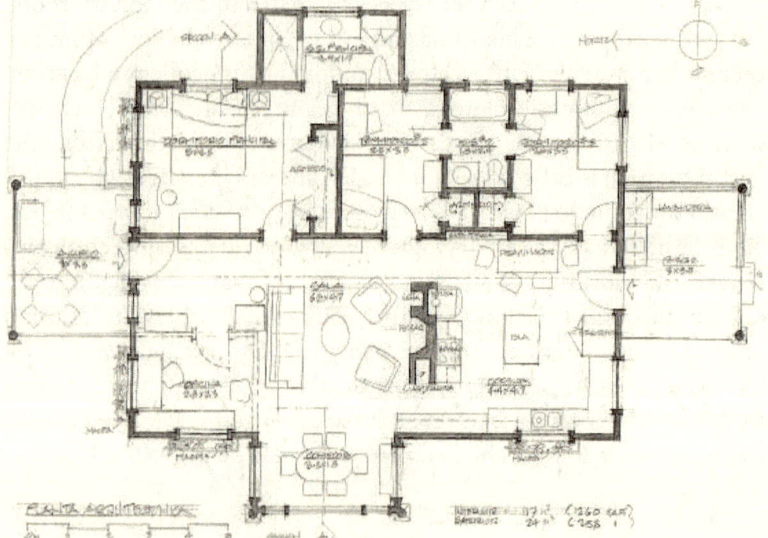

The Bonita Cabin has a huge laundry porch off the Kitchen for handy air drying in a delightful garden environment. Who says laundering cannot be fun?

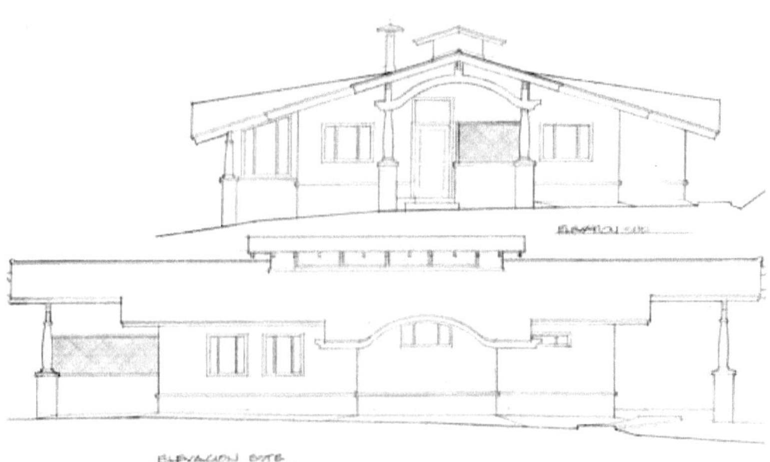

Chapter 26

Common Sense

As society becomes more complex, everything becomes specialized, and it seems that there are "experts" everywhere which are needed to figure anything out. The modern automobile would seem to be a magic device to someone from the Middle Ages. Open you own car's hood and look inside. Do you really think that you understand what is going on under there? If you say yes, you are either one of those "experts" or are deluding yourself. Complex societies tend to run up against entropy and drift apart into confusion. When this occurs, life needs to be simplified in order to get by.

So, what does this have to do with little houses? In a word, "simplify". The less complex one's lifestyle, the less difficult it is for us non-experts to do things for ourselves. Try cutting off your electrical circuits' breaker for a day and you will immediately face the reality I am referring to. The ideal house is also basic in its ability to help the occupants provide water, food, clothing and shelter. For any house, shelter is a given, and protection from the elements resulting in comfort is readily available with a modicum of thought. Security is another matter and realizing the astronomical firepower that any individual can hold in their hand, stone walls do not a fortress make. Little houses, the more humble, the better, are a psychological deterrent to thieves for the obvious reason. More sophisticated security measures are dealt with countless websites on the internet and beyond the scope of this book.

Clothing is a basic physical need which is easily and inexpensively provided in today's consumer society. Water, of course, is the most basic physical need and as such, has been attended to elsewhere in this book. Food production for personal consumption was, since the beginning of time, bonded to activities within and directly without the house. Gardening and home-based animal husbandry has gained significant interest recently and the concepts of "sustainability" and more specifically, Self Sufficiency Within Walking Distance will increasingly become integrated activities connected to life at home.

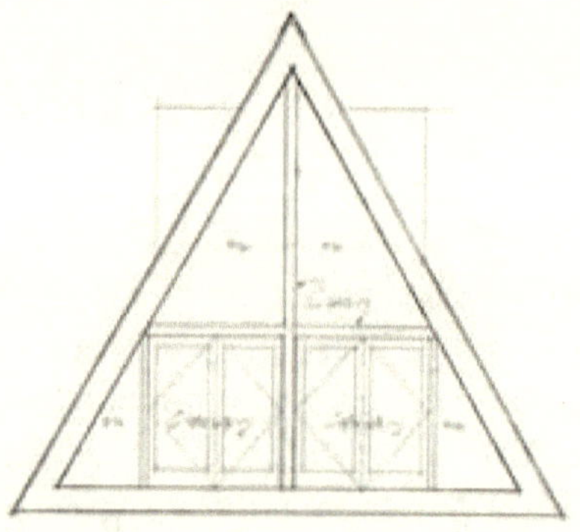

Delta Cabin

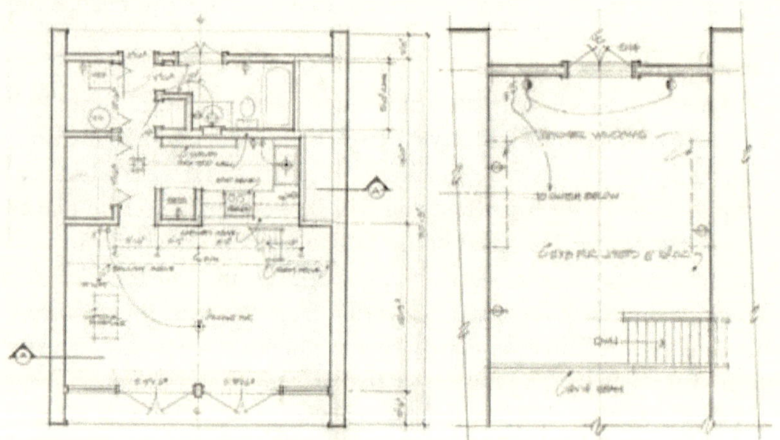

Ground Floor Plan   Loft Floor Plan

Delta Cabin is about as simple as this old crank has ever done. It was designed in 1970 as a demonstration "A" frame for a lumber company in the Ski Mountains of Colorado. Would I change it now that it is forty plus years later? For sure the twin double front doors would have to be traded out for a single one set off center right to accommodate a raised wainscot wall up to two feet high. This would mitigate the floor level freezing draft and allow for furniture placement adjacent to the front window. Also, an eyebrow window over the sink would offer a view and balanced natural light. Any design can be improved. It is important for the designer to be flexible, have common sense, and stick his ego in his back pocket.

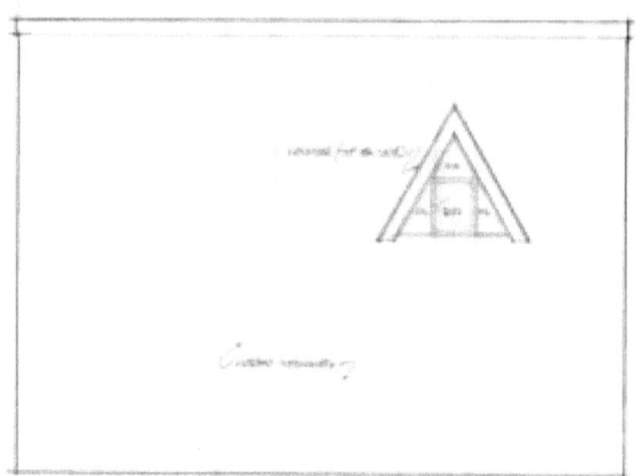

Left and Right-Side Elevation

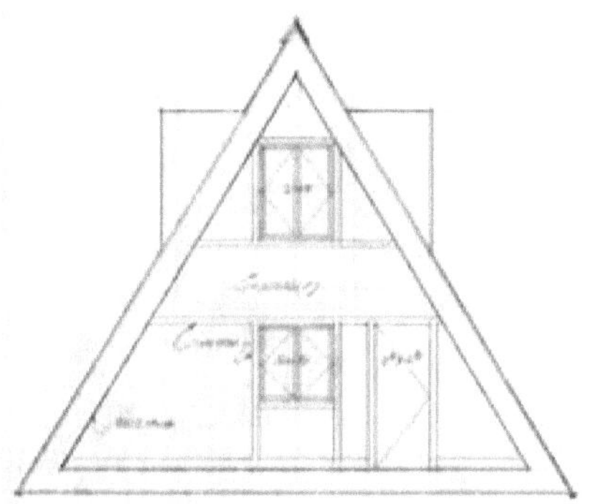

Rear Elevation

Delta Cabin has 620 square feet (58 sq. meters) interior livable floor area plus recommended front and back decks of 120 sq. ft. (11 m) each.

Chapter 27

Sustainability

There is a new religion in the Architectural world and its color is green. Don't get me wronged; the concept is a good one. Sustainable Architecture promotes the concept of efficiency within the built environment. To be sustainable, a building should be as efficient s possible regarding use of materials, use of energy, prevention of environmental waste and degradation, plus aid as a stage set for responsible behavior of the occupants. Most of the goals herein are straight forward and can be readily quantified into a "how to" list of commandments. Much research has been conducted to formulate a green catechism, establish a detailed code of ethics, and to assemble a priesthood called "LEEDS" (Leadership in Energy and environmental Design) to serve the faithful and admonish the transgressors.

Today you can readily locate an entire cohort of certified LEED'ers that will carefully design your new house to the absolute letter of the green dogma. Chances are, they will also design for you a boring box in the process. It is important to know that sustainability is not just a way of building, but a way of life. The richness of the spirit transcends just re-using the bricks and left-over tile. Every moment within a "sustainable" building should entice, enrich, uplift, enrapture, and produce a continuous sense of wonder. Nothing short of a holistic encounter is truly worthy of being called Green.

Western American Ranch

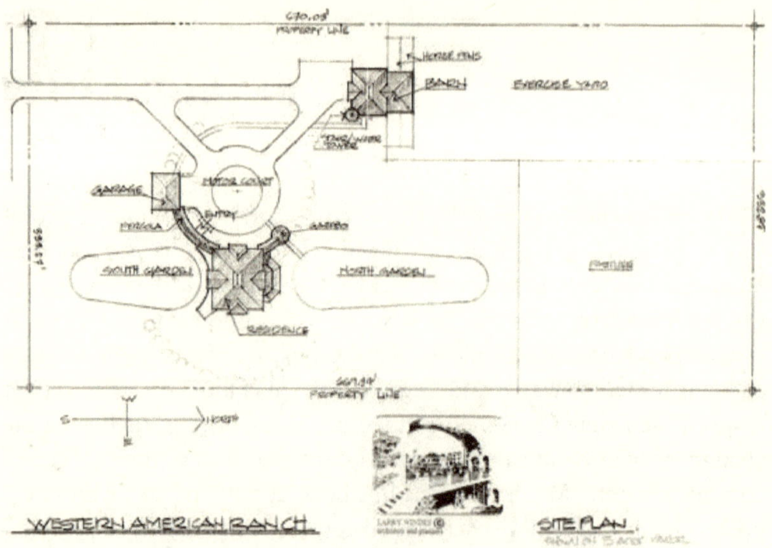

Here is a working horse ranch on five acres of land.

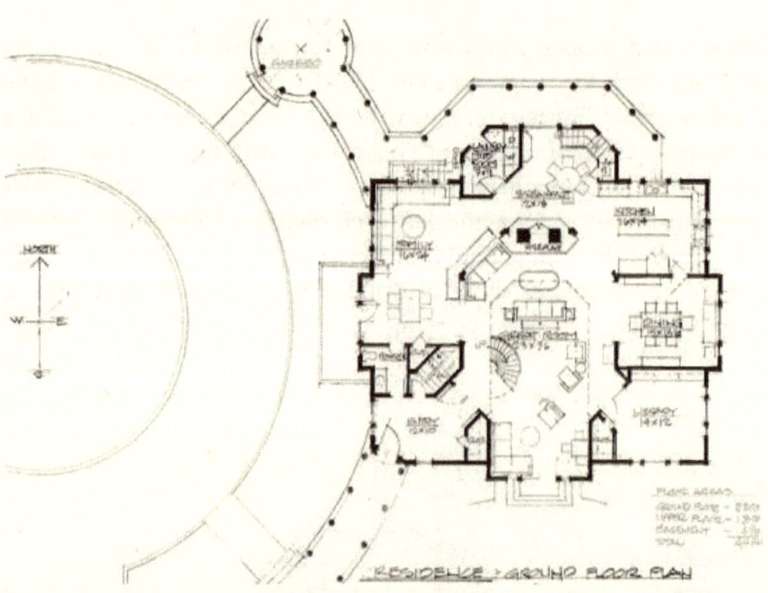

The two-story house is entered from a semi-circular breezeway connecting the garage. The circular breezeway motif continues around the house to a Gazebo and rear porch.

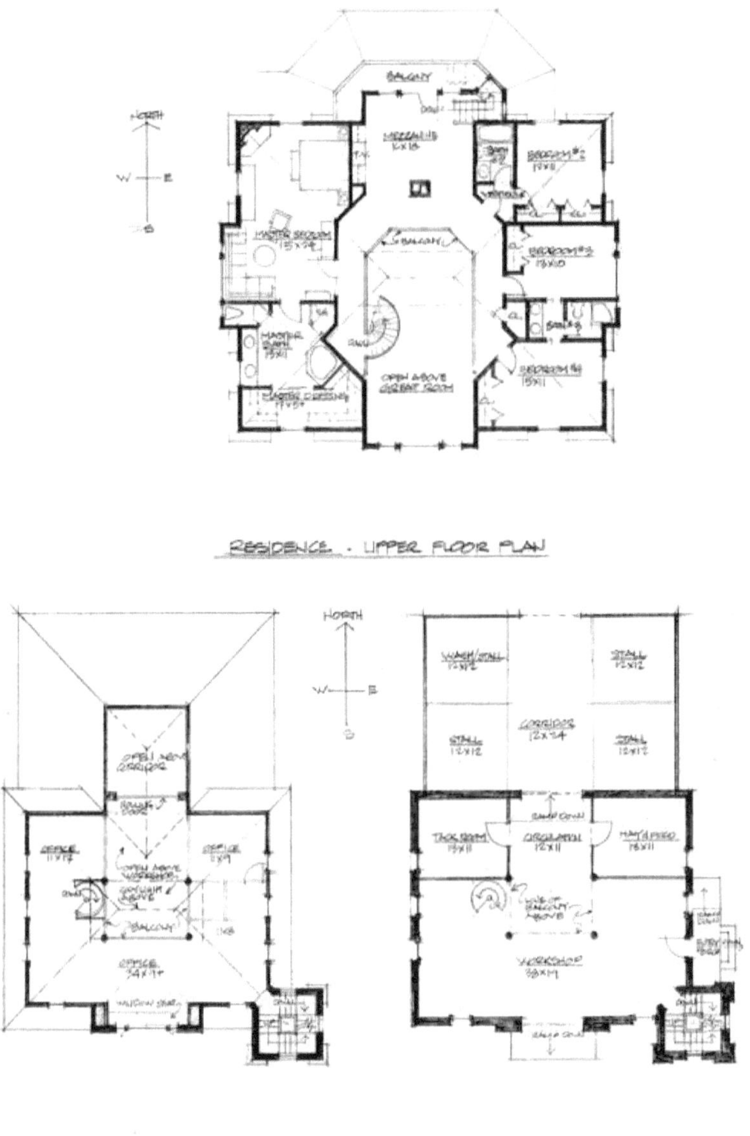

The Barn serves multiple functions. There are stalls and a wash area for the horses, a large workshop on the ground level, and offices on the mezzanine. At the top of the stair tower is located the water tank for the property.

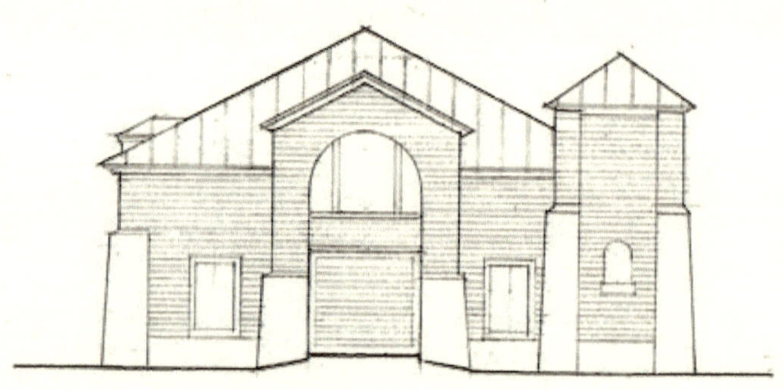

Although it may help to have five acres, a barn, corrals, and big house, self-sufficiency relates to what activities are undertaken by the inhabitants. On an acre of land next to a stream and nestling under the arms of a two-hundred-year-old Cocobola (Rosewood) tree, Casa Laura provides all the necessary attributes for a sustainable lifestyle.

Casa Laura

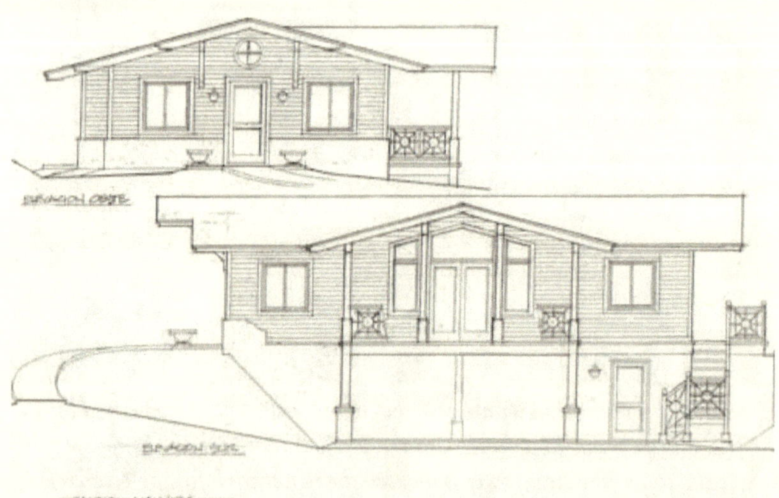

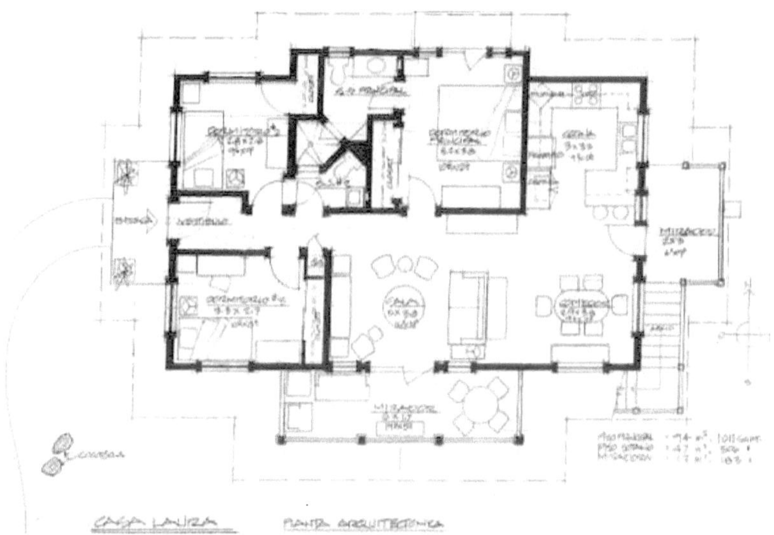

Casa Laura can be built on a flat or gently sloping site as a single level or as shown on the elevations with a basement walk-out level double carport and laundry. At a mere thousand square feet livable floor area (93 sq. m), there are three bedrooms, two baths which share a single shower plus generous kitchen/Dining/Living areas within a flowing space. The Ouest (West) Elevation shows a classic Costa Rica farmhouse façade updated for contemporary times. Generous roof overhangs and Miradors (terraces) on all sides allow for easy indoor-outdoor living within the tropical cloud forest climate 9 degrees above the Equator.

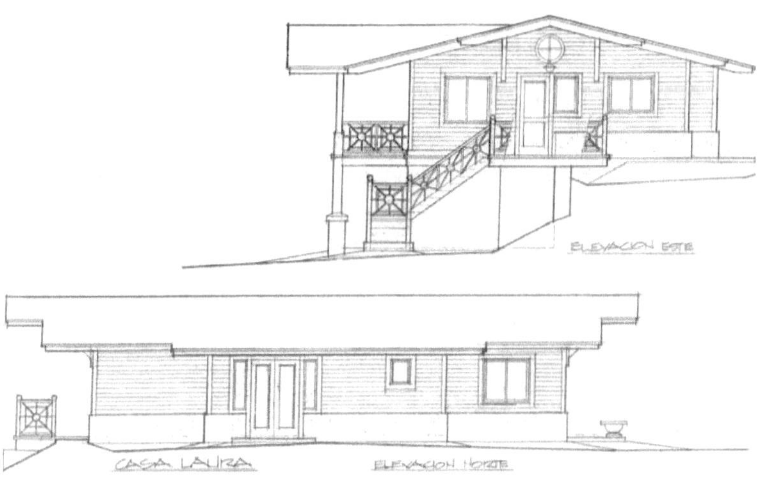

Casa Carmen

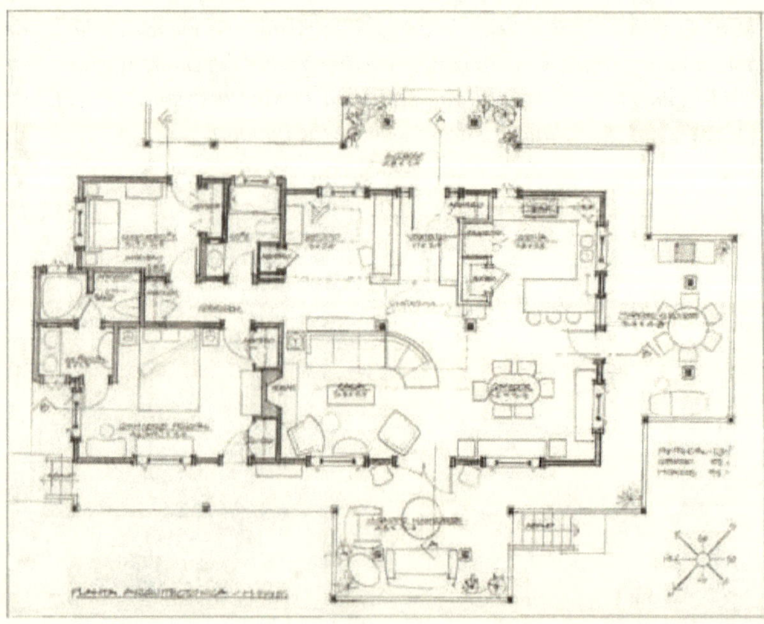

In a tropical climate, wide roof overhangs curb moisture on exterior walls and allow for a dry pathway around the house. By extending the overhangs even further, a perimeter porch provides year-round outside living spaces. The only drawback is the interior central rooms tend to be a bit gloomy even with adequate window sizes. The answer is a roof mounted cupola (claraboya) with surrounding clerestory windows that bathes the entire living areas with bright sunlight.

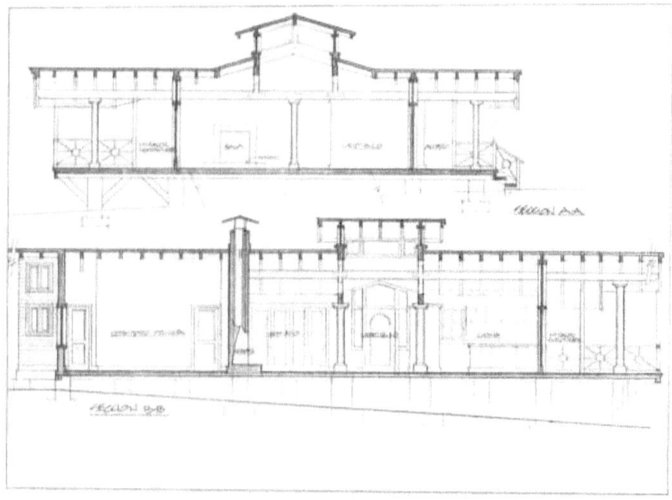

Casa Carmen contains 1216 square feet (113 sq. meters) of livable area; 1022 sq. ft. (95 sq. m.) covered porches (miradors), and a detached two car garage with laundry (Lavanderia)/storage (bodega) rooms. The Master Bedroom Suite (dormitorio principal) opens to a compartmented dressing/bath with whirlpool. The second bedroom (dormitorio #2) has a ships ladder that provides vertical access to a hideaway above the Master Dressing/Bath. This small room doubles as a sleeping loft and storage area. The Studio (estudio) enjoys the clerestory natural light and is open to the living area. The Studio functions as a 3rd Bedroom/Guestroom when the disappearing doors are closed, and the Murphy bed is opened.

The cross section (seccion) drawings show a raised floor system that is particularly effective on sloping or uneven terrain especially when constant ground moisture is problematic. Individually poured concrete pads dug into the earth support 18" (45 cm) diameter precast concrete pipes which have attached diagonal supports extending to a hardwood frame. Over the frame hardwood decking is added at the miradors. The interior is concrete block with a poured concrete floor and wood frame walls and roof.

The building structure above may also incorporate steel, wood, masonry or any other required materials as desired.

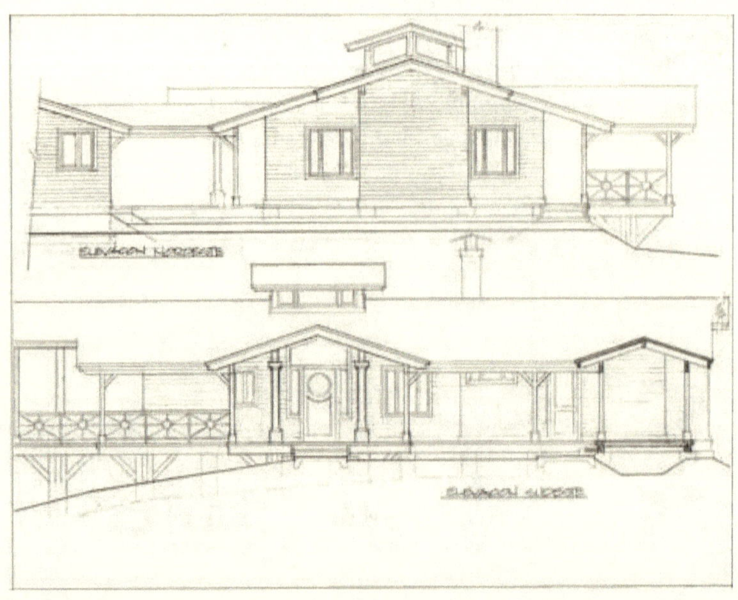

An open breezeway separates the house and garage (cobertizo para automoviles) and does double duty as a laundry drying area.

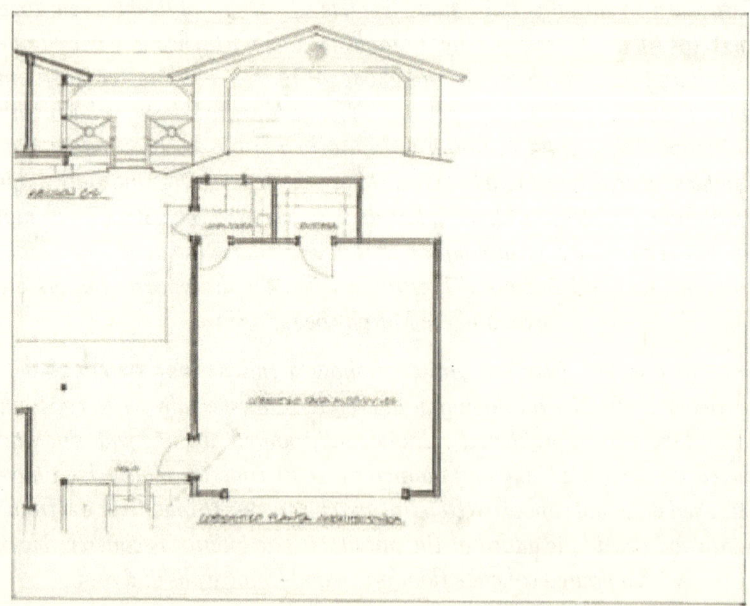

Casa Maria

As you arrive at this juncture in the book, the focus on A Grand Life within a Tiny House is now offered to you. Casa Maria was built on a beautiful working avocado farm overlooking Hush Valley in Costa Rica. At an elevation of nearly 8,000 feet (2,400 meters) in a tropical cloud forest, this small weekend vacation home declares its presence as if to say, "Though I am tiny, yet I am Grand."

To accommodate the sloping site, the ground floor and soaring front porch hover above the single carport and embrace the view of the valley below. With only a footprint of a mere 880 square feet (82 square meters), Casa Maria's unique high center roof ridge line and upwardly curved roof eaves, provide a spacious interior with natural light coming from all directions. The 200 square feet (18 square meter) loft is both airy and cozy while four people are asleep. Together with a queen-sized bed in the bedroom, a sofa bed in the Living Room, plus the Loft, eight persons are sleeping comfortably. The bathroom provides a tub/shower combination. The kitchen includes a stove top, a microwave oven, a under counter refrigerator and a single sink. There is a laundry/storage room under the ground floor. Although air conditioning is not necessary in this climate, a 250-year-old Rumford designed metal fireplace in the Living Room augments to remove the morning chill. Casa Maria's large roof overhangs effectively sheds the ample rainfall away from the walls, even though the entire area under the roof is only 750 square feet (70 square meters).

The attached photos demonstrate the author's site-built version of what a truly livable Tiny House can be. What do you think?

Here is a pencil drawing of Casa Maria from the driveway below.

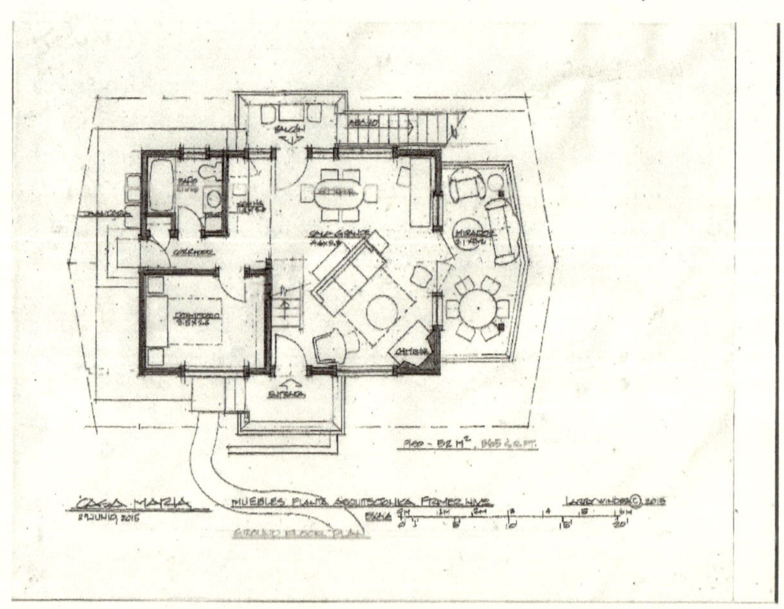

The Ground Floor Plan shows a Floor area of 565 square feet (52 sq. m).

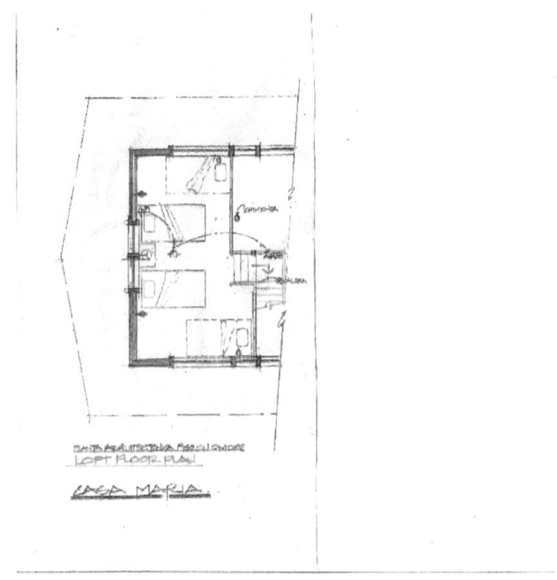

The Loft Floor Area is 200 square feet (19 sq.m).

As built, Casa Maria demonstrates the same visual presence as the drawing.

From the hillside above, Casa Maria nestles into the avocado orchard.

The metal fireplace is filled with sand to retain the heat. The original design is from the late 1700's by Benjamin Thompson who promulgated the most efficient geometry for wood burning fireplaces. He designed more than a million fireplaces throughout the London environs and was elevated to the peerage as Count Rumford.

The interior space is lit naturally via the highly pitched roof and soaring rounded side window walls.

Chapter 28

Self Sufficiency within Walking Distance

After boiling down much of the "Green" hype and Sustainable dogma, just what could be the outcome of a sensible and holistic endeavor regarding a building to live in and a lifestyle within it? My personal quest as an architect, planner, and builder for more than fifty years can be summed up as "self-sufficiency within walking distance." The concept of providing the most basic needs, water, food, clothing and shelter may be a bit of a stretch in the literal sense. Mom is not going to immediately run out, put on a strap loom, and start weaving an Alpaca bedspread. But she just might start a kitchen garden full of vegetables and herbs. Dad might forgo the final nine and actually walk back home from the 19th green. The kids might even shut off the social network for an extra thirty minutes to ride a bicycle to the soccer game. More time spent at home means less time-wasting gas, especially if the family plans in advance to eliminate one stop shopping. Since the lawn boy moved back to Mexico, Junior may attempt the intricacies of the lawn mower, to say nothing of the weed eater. Heaven forbids, Sis may become mistress of the laundry room. A hundred years ago, children were a worthwhile commodity and worked (worked?) alongside their parents to assist supporting the livelihood of the family. During this process children learned variable skills that would enable them to create true worth plus generate an ethic of positive accomplishment and self-respect.

Does any of this have meaning today? Be your own judge. Not everyone wants or needs to be a subsistence farmer. Since real estate sales, skilled manufacturing, sensible financial services, skilled construction, artistry, and numerous other endeavors seem to be less needed or are outsourced across international borders, the thought of becoming a bit more personally reliant could save time and money. Growing a home garden not only provides healthy nourishment for your waistline but allows direct participation in a timeless creation of poetry for the soul. Little, sensible houses, especially without a mortgage, are the cornerstone of the family. The neighborhood can be the most direct support group, providing one exercises the "walking distance" aspect and gets to know the people next door since, chances are, there is a shopping center within a half mile away. If you walk to pick-up those next grocery items, not only will your heart rate thank you, but you will purchase fewer impulse goodies, especially the second time around. At risk of being a continuous bore, I will leave you with the following personal observation.

Fifteen years ago, my lovely wife, Cindy, and I moved to the coffee mountains of Costa Rica and began a dedicated odyssey toward an increasingly self-sufficient lifestyle. Having preached about it for years, we are finally doing it. No car, nearly no money, but a perfect climate and a region rife with competent subsistence farmers next door, we are "living like ancient royalty" (the no car bit) and loving every minute.

Here is Cindy standing over the kitchen sink and looking out the window towards the lovely Mountain View while enjoying another day of a Grand Life.

Chapter 29

To the Future

Much of this book was written ten years ago. Most of the houses shown here were completed more than five years ago. Since then, have people's attitudes towards their future objectives changed?

Our market research records comments by potential future buyers. "I am extremely curious." "I am looking forward to my future adventures." "These homes offer the best incentive for cash. A great alternative considering all the environmental changes." "I don't have a Tiny House yet, but have discovered that building (or having someone build) a Tiny House is half the battle, because, at the end of the day, the Tiny House is no good to me if I can't find somewhere safe, affordable, and pleasant to 'park' it."

Yes!

We have heard from you.

To The Future, we offer our version of a Tiny House for living and working within. The name of this Tiny House is "Fold-A-Mansion," and for short, "FAM".

Today, FAM resides within the beautiful mountains of Costa Rica. Tomorrow, FAM could be located anywhere. Here to follow, are descriptions, drawings, and photos of various versions of FAM to welcome your Grand Life.

As a final thought, when Cindy and I moved to Costa Rica, it was all about our independence and freedom. It is so amazing to live and work where you want to be. To be your own boss. Within the FAM concept, if it feels wrong, just pack everything together and park it somewhere else. Meet other independent and free people up the road. Build a community of like-minded people and follow your heart.

We did and are eternally grateful.

Super Fold-A-Mansion III

The tiny house movement has gone viral the world over. The idea of being able to have a complete home that can be towed behind a vehicle, although not new, is a timely concept. With the cost of full-sized homes being beyond the reach of many, coupled with the high cost of land, the future requires another alternative. THOW's (Tiny House on Wheels) have offered practical solutions to the cost problem. Also, the portability allows a mobile populace to take their home along with them. Virtually all these houses are designed to conform to highway legal status of 8½' width, 13½' height and 26' plus length. The resulting interior space is limited, however, and after a week or two within these cramped spaces, claustrophobia often sets in. Wouldn't it be grand if your tiny 200 square foot (19 sq. meters) could be parked and then more than doubled in size to contain a real kitchen, full bath with tub/shower, ample living/dining area, and two full bedroom areas, plus a sleeping loft?

Now you can with "Fold-A-Mansion". This lightweight and heavily insulated THOW does all this and more. Not only does it have twice the floor and cubic area of a standard 26' long THOW, but it also contains a real "U" shaped kitchen. The kitchen sports a 24" refrigerator, 24" range/oven, 18" dishwasher, microwave, sink and countertop bar with space for three stools. The bathroom has a full bathtub/shower (with optional whirlpool), and there is space for a combination clothes washer/dryer in the cabinet of the Master Bedroom area.

The Master Bedroom sleeps two within a Double Size bed plus a wardrobe closet. Bedroom #2 area contains a single Murphy combination bed/desk. The sleeping "Pop-Up" (with 5'-6" headroom) loft contains a Queen size bed, and with an optional sofa/bed in the Living Room, FAM-II allows a total of 7 persons to sleep in comfort.

The Fold-A-Mansion offers the complete range of features for off-grid living as optional accessories.

The Fold-A-Mansion also incorporates a most valuable feature, rarely ever seen, on a THOW. Most exterior walls and covered porches are provided with a minimum 2-foot-wide roof overhang. This provides comfort and cleanliness, especially in wet climates.

The Fold-A-Mansion conversion process is easily folded open and closed by professionals and readily leveled for use as any standard THOW.

<u>SUPER Fold-A-Mansion III</u> is the truly "big sized" tiny house. 2022

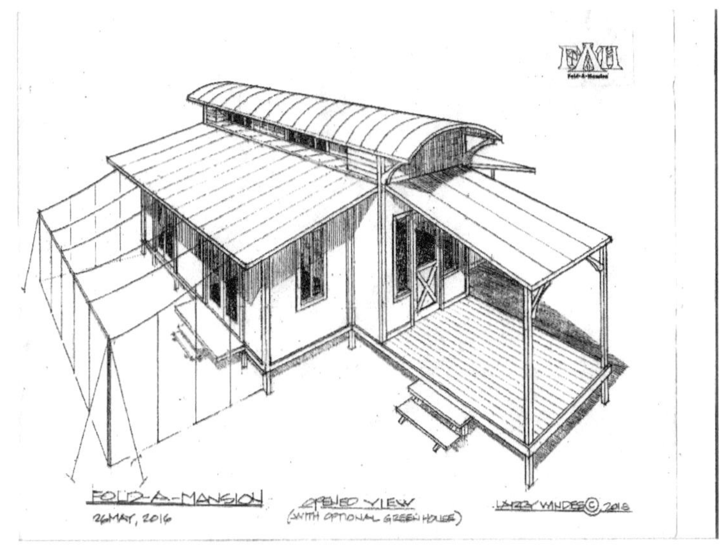

This perspective drawing shows the first FAM in the opened view, together with an optional plastic greenhouse tent attached to one side.

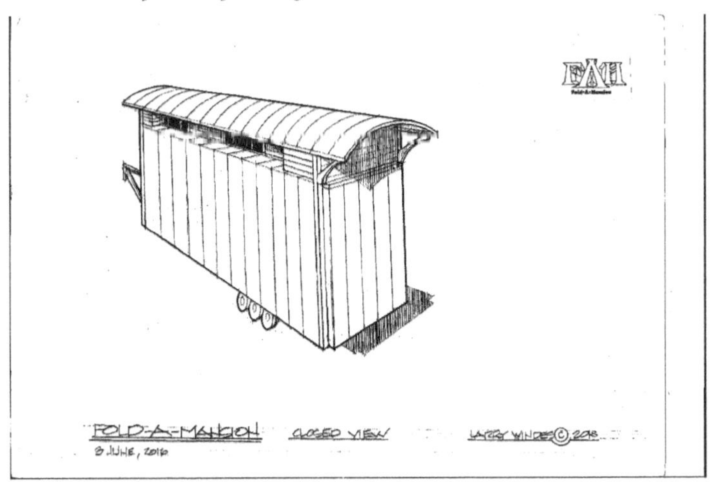

When fully closed and ready for relocation, FAM is street legal within most locations around the world.

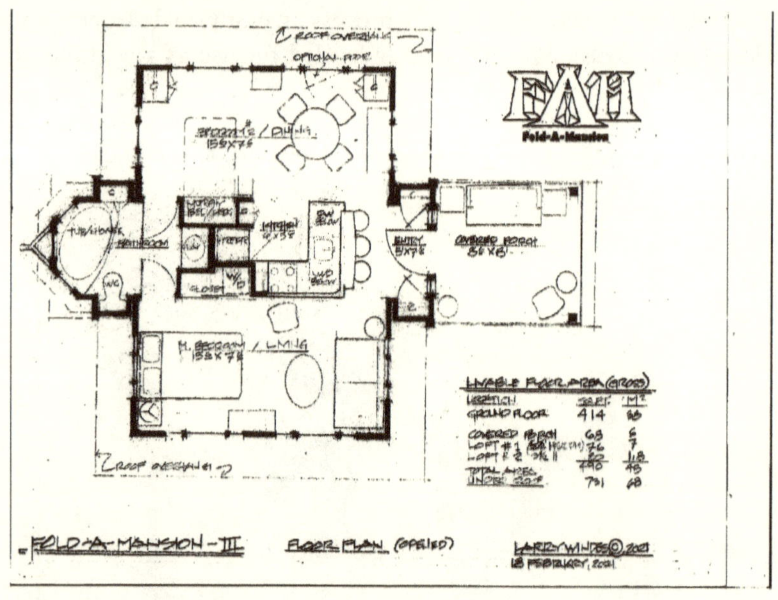

When opened, FAM has a spacious open plan with numerous windows facing all directions.

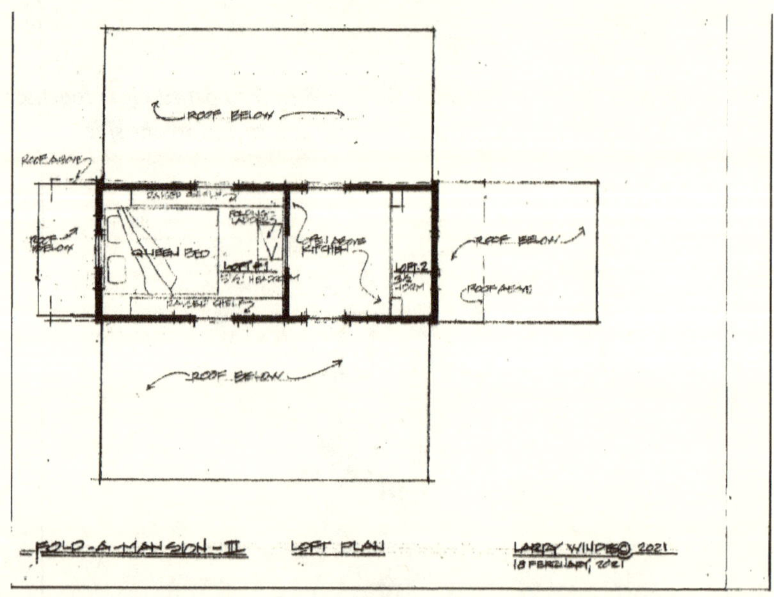

FAM Pop-Up Loft has a 5'6" (1.68 m) clear headroom and 7 windows facing 4 different directions.

In a glance, the difference between FAM and nearly ALL other Tiny Houses is here, and it is the roof overhangs. FAM only looks like a Shipping container Box when it is folded up and on the road. When FAM is opened, it is spacious, inside and out.

FAM accommodates various ground levels while embracing rain sheltered decks.

Just inside the front door, Mauricio and the little one is watching as Laura stands at the Kitchen sink between the dishwasher and the range/oven. The interior open space shown here is more than 20' (6m) across.

The Living/Master Bedroom area shows a double bed with views of the coffee plantation.

The Living area view shows the Kitchen on the left, Entry beyond, and the Front covered porch through the window. The air conditioning unit is on the small loft above the entry door.

Here is Laura standing on the Queen size bed within the Pop-Up Loft. Ample headroom and spacious area will accommodate a real bedroom or office with ample light and views.

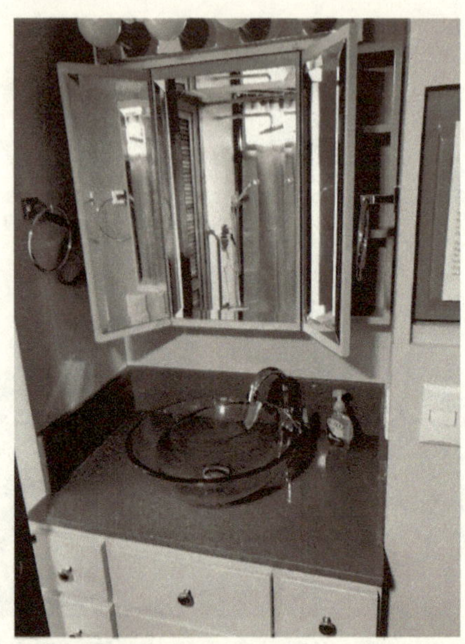

The Bathroom has a quartz topped vanity with a clear glass lavatory and a triple mirrored upper cabinet. Now the ladies can see all three sides with a single view.

FAM has a spacious whirlpool tub/ shower combination. Are you ready to move in yet?

Super Fold-A-Mansion "Take Away Resort."

When contemplating the creation of a new business, location is always at the forefront. This is especially so when a new business requires the construction of new buildings. Should the location prove to be wrong, the entire business could be doomed. What if that loss can be prevented by allowing the business to immediately and cheaply relocate to another location? What if an entire Resort / Hotel project with numerous buildings can be folded up and moved quickly and easily on public highways? What if the initial construction cost of the project is within the parameters of quality site-built buildings? There is no "If."

The Fold-A-Mansion products are a series of modular buildings that are prefabricated, then folded up to become street legal for transportation to the building site. Once they arrive at the site location, they are easily folded open by professionals and readily leveled for use. All the various resorts uses, i. e. Reception, Café, Bar, Suites, Hotel Rooms, assembly venues, Services, Storage, Staff housing, etc. are custom designed to be incorporated within the FAM concept. Additionally, any other use may also be accommodated, such as office, school, clinic, home, shop, fast food, etc.

The basic modules can be designed not only to accommodate virtually any use, they also may be designed to conform to whatever visual character that is desired by the purchaser, subject to size and weight considerations. The Fam concept also allows for incorporating various combinations of sustainability platforms, including complete off-grid features as optional accessories.

Permanence and portability are now effectively blended within the FAM concept. An entire tiny house community may result within the FAM concept, where location independence is the wave of the future.

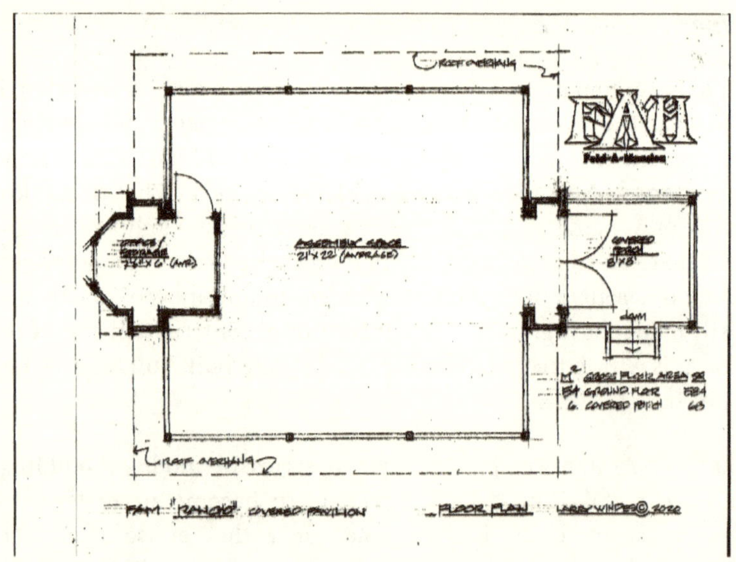

In Costa Rica an assembly building is referred to as a "Rancho." As a multi-use pavilion, it can readily be adapted for a myriad of quickly changed uses.

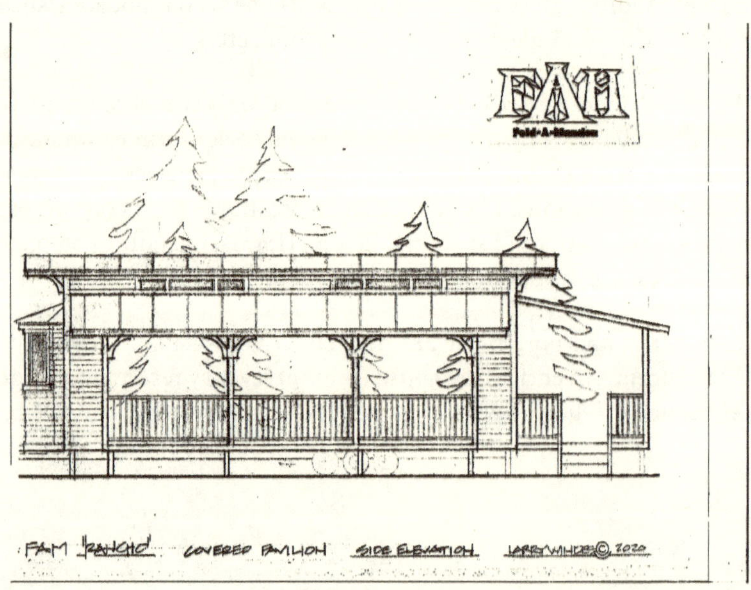

The FAM Rancho can be built as an open-air covered space or as an air-conditioned building.

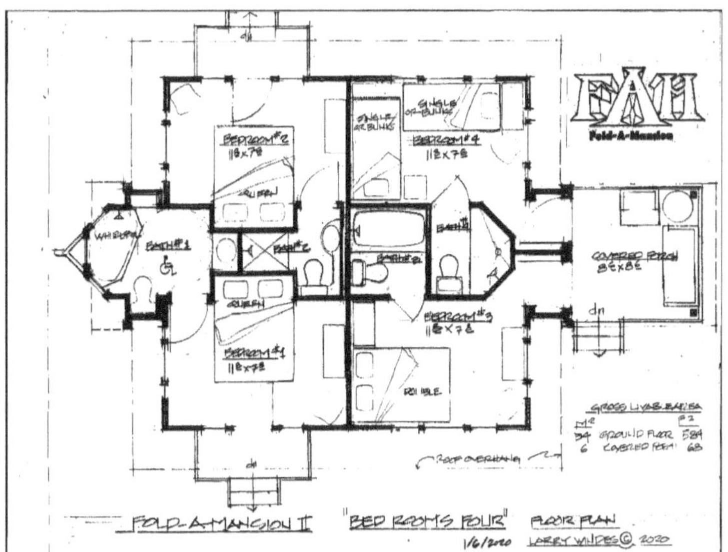

Here are four Bedroom suites with bath incorporated within a single FAM. By simply adding as many of these FAM's as required, growing needs are readily accommodated.

By assembling numerous FAMs to include virtually any combination of uses, an entire community can be placed on a single site area and quickly removed and relocated when need arises.

For transporting, all of FAM folds up with exception of this balcony/stairs and the stairs at the front entry, which are unbolted and carried within a truck which is towing FAM.

Coffee Marketing Concepts with FAM

Vertical integration is not a new concept. Common sense dictates that the producer of any product can keep the highest price in the house, if there are fewer middlemen between the producer and the retail buyer. Many coffee farmers in the world today process their own green coffee themselves with micro-mills, but they are still in need of numerous „middlemen" to offshore and market their coffee. If the farmer can reach the final buyer, either to sell roasted packaged coffee or, even better, „By the Cup ", the farmer will have the opportunity to realize the optimum financial return.

Large and successful companies around the world sell coffee to the retail market within three primary venues.

Coffee Kiosk
Coffee Trailer
Coffee Shop

All three of these locations offer brewed coffee and packaged coffee for the consumer to take home. These three vary in size and location depending upon the niche market that is targeted. They also vary in initial cost for construction, set-up, and operation.

1. Coffee Kiosk: This sales platform is small, 8' x 10' (2.5m x 3m), is usually operated by a single person, and often located within a large grocery store, shopping mall, or on a sidewalk. Kiosks located within a building usually obtain electrical, water and waste plumbing from the landlord but do not require a waterproof enclosure. They are usually prefabricated and moved to their service location on the back of a flatbed truck. They are easily and inexpensively relocated should the market area not be sufficient for prosperity.

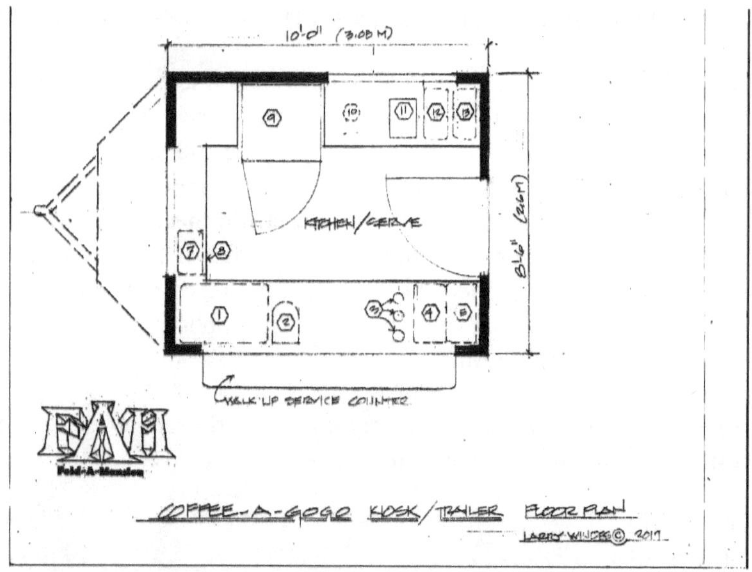

2. Coffee Trailer: A Coffee Trailer is like the Kiosk with the exception that it resides upon a set of wheels, is pulled by a vehicle, and functions within an environmentally weatherproof enclosure. The Coffee Trailer only requires sufficient exterior space to locate and for walk-up customer access. It can be connected to external water, power, and sewer, or can be designed to be internally self-sufficient. Being street legal, the Coffee Trailer is also easily able to relocate to "Take the Cup to the Customer." The Coffee Trailer may also include within, a small bathroom and sleeping loft to provide living accommodations for the operator.

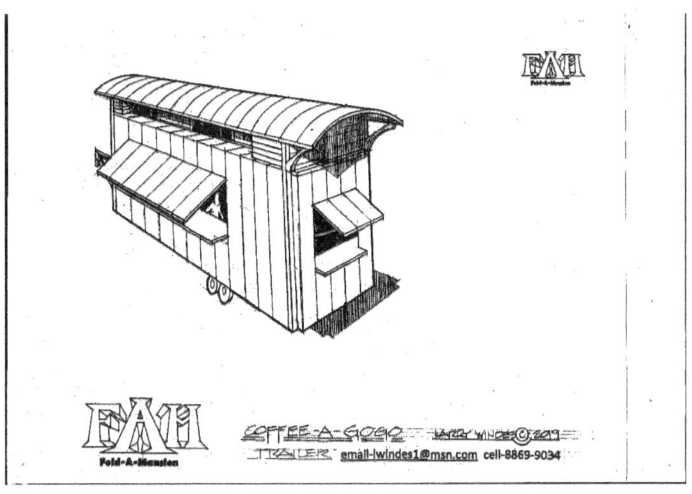

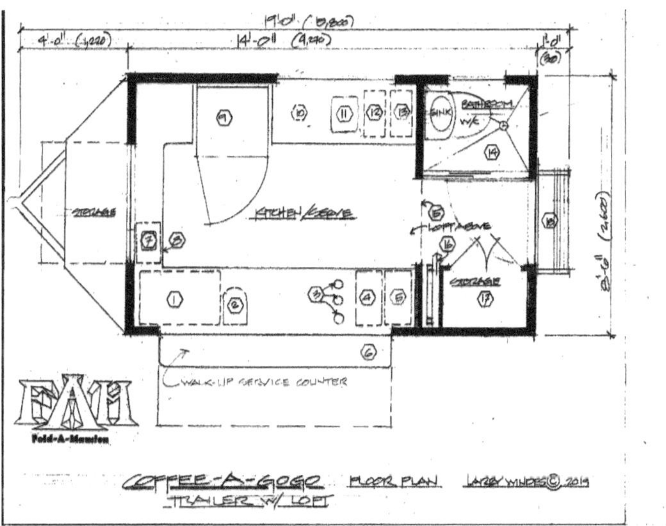

3. Coffee Shop: There are millions of Coffee Shops of every size and description throughout the world. Generally, they occupy stand-alone buildings or are located within commercial retail spaces. Coffee Shops are the most expensive of the three venues and require thoughtful planning to assess the market location. Due to the permanent nature of the facility, if the cup is taken to the location and there are NOT enough customers, oooops? The wrong location can be extremely costly and result in a potential business failure.

Unless - Your Coffee Shop is a "FAM", an independent business on wheels.

The "FAM" Fold-A-Mansion Coffee Shop absolutely solves the market location problem. FAM is a thirty customer Coffee Shop which starts out as a street legal trailer, and upon arrival, folds out to become a complete building. The FAM Coffee Shop contains two dining rooms, a covered entry porch, full kitchen, and handicapped accessible service rooms for women and men. FAM may also be fully off-grid for power using optional equipment. Now even the best of both worlds allows the owner to have a small business and tiny house all rolled into one single FAM.

FAM incorporates a sleeping loft and shower where staff accommodation is prudent and allowed by governing rules. Once again, FAM Coffee Shop can be folded up within a few hours and towed to another location. Truly the FAM Coffee Shop takes the Cup to the Customer ".

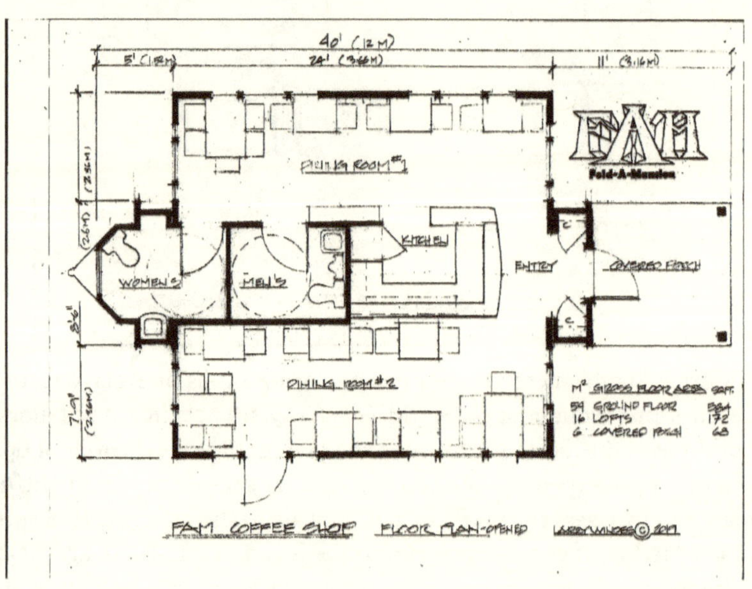

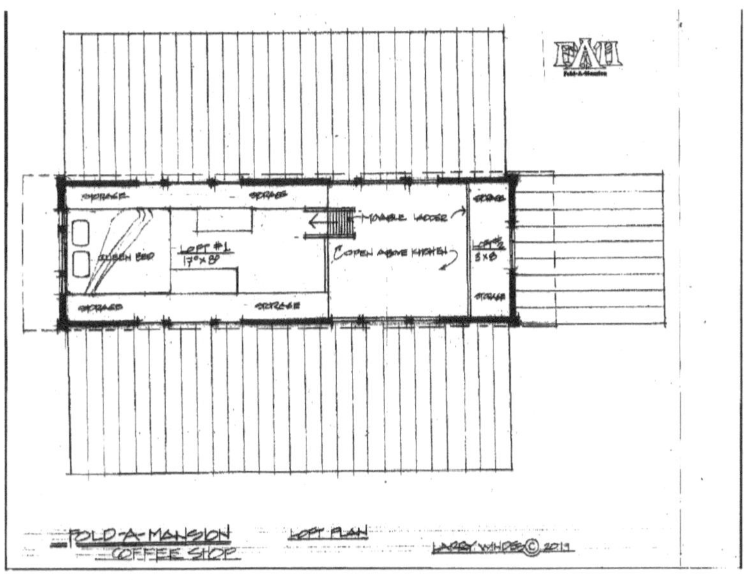

FAM Coffee Shop Entry Porch offers pleasant outdoor dining.

Interior Dining Room #1 embraces comfortable dining and gracious views.

Another view of Dining Room #1 shows the Kitchen and Entry area plus the Covered Entry Porch beyond.

Dining Room #2 is on the opposite side of the Kitchen with similar views.

Friends greeting friends on the Covered Front Porch.

Away We Go

Freedom, Freedom, Freedom is just a FAM away. So, you always have craved adventure. So, you always wanted to be your own boss. So, you have always had a sense of wonder.

FAM can help you expand your horizons. Live, work, play, exercise, meditate, meet friends, delight within nature. All is available to you should you just decide. FAM not only allows you to reside anywhere, but that anywhere, can change, as your wishes change, while still retaining your personal sense of place. The life of freedom can still be Grand, together with FAM.

Index of Plans by Floor Area

Floor area less than 1000 square feet (93sq. meters)

Plan	Floor Area (square feet)	Floor Area (square meters)
The Smallest House	320	30
Anne's Cabin	375	35
FAM-III	490	46
Tica Cottage	524	48
Delta Cabin	620	58
Alta Chalet	672	62
Alpine Cabin	712	66
Casa Maria	800	74
Rustico Cabin-1 story	807	75
Rustico Cabin-w/ topknot	919	85
Guesthouse over a Garage (apt. only)	960	89
Eloquencia Cottage	974	90
Casa Adriana	990	92

Floor area 1000 – 1500 square feet (93 – 139m2))

Casa Laura	*1011*	*94*
Cathy's Cabin	*1100*	*102*
Casa Emily	*1200*	*108*
Casa Carmen	*1216*	*113*
Bonita Cabin	*1260*	*117*
Alta Duplex (total for two)	*1344*	*125*
Villa "C"	*1410*	*131*

Floor area 1501 – 2000 square feet (140 – 186m2)

Vanessa's Lighthouse	*1580*	*147*
Casa Jeanne	*1590*	*148*
Dale's House	*1596*	*148*
Rustico Cabin – 2 story	*1610*	*149*
Kay's Cottage	*1650*	*153*
Villa 'B'	*1665*	*155*
Villa 'A'	*1700*	*158*
Villa 'J'	*1745*	*162*
Bella Cabin	*1782*	*165*

Floor area 2001 – 3000 square Feet (187 – 279m2)

Cynthia's Manor	2040	189
Villa 'H'	2070	192
The Tower	2260	210
Classic Cottage	2274	211
Villa 'M'	2356	219
Kathryn's High Victorian	2420	226
Oasis Villa	2490	231
Mountain Villa	2496	232
Villa 'P'	2528	235
Mountain Cottage	2560	238
Villa 'K'	2611	243
Desert Deco	2650	247
Villa 'R'	2801	260

Floor area 3001 Plus (279 plus m2)

Cynthia Manor w/lower ground floor	3240	301
Western American Ranch	4480	416
Paradise Manor	5700	530

About the Author & the Architect

Larry Windes was born with a passion to create the environment we live in. From stacking up little rock houses in the front yard, covering the living room furniture with bed sheet tents, delighting in Lincoln Log houses, that compulsion led to drafting class in high school, then Bachelor of Architecture degree at Arizona State University.

Upon obtaining his professional architectural license, he founded his firm in Aspen, Colorado, USA in the early 1970's where he specialized in the creation of innovative physical environments utilizing inspiration from the past, present, and the future. Moving to Manhattan, New York he pioneered the Festival Market concept by executing the Master Plan and Design of BridgeMarket under the approaches to the Queensborough Bridge in 1975.

The architect has continued design, planning, and development tasks in Arizona, Colorado, California, New York, and Hawaii within the USA, plus Great Britain, France, Spain, Saudi Arabia, and Egypt. After completing the master plan and design of Eloy City, a 10,000-acre city of 35,000 population in Arizona, enough was enough. Together with his lovely wife Cynthia, they semi-retired to the coffee mountains of Costa Rica.

WEBSITE: WWW.LARRYWINDES.COM

EMAIL: LWINDES1@MSN.COM

PHONE: 506 (COSTA RICA) 8869-9034

www.ingramcontent.com/pod-product-compliance
Lightning Source LLC
Chambersburg PA
CBHW020950160726

47994CB00006B/2151